PRAISE FOR *HOW TO TALK TO CUSTOMERS*

"I hope you believe in MAGIC, because this system can really help you build the generous, intimate, personal relationships with customers that will power the growth of your business!"

> —Keith Ferrazzi, author, *Never Eat Alone,* and CEO of professional development and consulting firm Ferrazzi Greenlight

"If you deal with people, this book is a must-have! The relationships with your 'customers' (clients, coworkers, family, and friends) will flourish as you put MAGIC to work."

> —Jason Checketts, manager of learning and development, Wells Fargo

"There's no greater way to help your team build a culture of customer service than by using the MAGIC system. You'll see results immediately . . . and those results will truly amaze you (and your customers!)."

> —Brian Cole Miller, author, *Quick Team-Building Activities for Busy Managers*

"MAGIC is one of those simple-but-far-from-easy ideas that can revolutionize a company because it transforms how people think and act. At FreshDirect, we believe in MAGIC and strive to practice it daily."

> —Dean Furbush, CEO, FreshDirect

"Any call center senior executive, manager, supervisor—or anyone who talks to your customers—should read this book then commit to applying its simple principles. Tom and Diane bring to light the fact that all consumers are seeking a unique experience from companies today, and this is it."

> —C. Paul Turner, managing director, Training and Performance Improvement, Citifinancial Mortgage, Inc., and Citicorp Trust Bank, fsb

"Any organization interested in creating passionate and loyal customers should read this book. The MAGIC system shows you how to impress even the most discerning customers."

> —Rudy Escalante, CEO, ICSA Software North America, Inc.

JB JOSSEY-BASS

How to Talk to Customers

CREATE A GREAT IMPRESSION
EVERY TIME WITH MAGIC

Diane Berenbaum
Tom Larkin

Jes,
Hope you find
this helpful.

Diane Berenbaum

Tom Larkin

John Wiley & Sons, Inc.

Published by Jossey-Bass
A Wiley Imprint
989 Market Street, San Francisco, CA 94103-1741   www.josseybass.com

Jossey-Bass books and products are available through most bookstores. To contact Jossey-Bass directly call our Customer Care Department within the U.S. at 800-956-7739, outside the U.S. at 317-572-3986, or fax 317-572-4002.

Jossey-Bass also publishes its books in a variety of electronic formats. Some content that appears in print may not be available in electronic books.

Library of Congress Cataloging-in-Publication Data
Berenbaum, Diane, 1956–
  How to talk to customers : create a great impression every time with MAGIC / Diane Berenbaum, Tom Larkin.
       p. cm.
  Includes bibliographical references.
  ISBN 978-0-7879-8752-7 (cloth)
1. Customer relations. 2. Interpersonal relations. I. Larkin, Tom, 1953– II. Title.
  HF5415.5.B445 2007
  658.8'12—dc22   2006101788

Printed in the United States of America
FIRST EDITION
HB Printing   10 9 8 7 6 5 4 3 2

In memory of Bobbie Chila,

who epitomized the spirit of MAGIC and never wavered,

and

To our clients and certified facilitators around the globe,

who bring MAGIC to life in their organizations.

This book could not have been written without you.

CONTENTS

PREFACE

It seems so simple, yet it is rare. In fact, we're still surprised when it happens.

When you answer the phone, it's nice if you sound like you are having a great day. Sound like you are happy to hear from me. When I walk into your store, look me in the eye and offer a genuine smile. Greet me as you would like to be greeted.

It seems so simple. So why are examples like these the exception rather than the norm?

The late Buckminster Fuller, American visionary, designer, architect, and inventor of the geodesic dome, was one of these great exceptions. Ten minutes shy of giving a speech to thousands of people in a huge auditorium, he had disappeared. Finally someone found him in the public restroom. He was picking up trash off the floor and wiping the counters around the sinks. The person said to him, "Mr. Fuller, what are you doing? Aren't you speaking in ten minutes?"

He replied, "Oh, I'm just cleaning my bathroom."

Whose world is it? Whose responsibility is it to make it a place where we like to be? Bucky felt it was his. And we feel it is ours.

Can actions like Bucky's become the norm? We think so. This book was written because we are passionate about *interpersonal sustainability*. We believe in treating each other in such a way that our actions make a positive contribution to another's day. Every interpersonal contact should contribute to the desire to be in a continued relationship with the other party.

We'd love to think about what *that* could do for business, and for mankind.

It seems so simple.

We actually believe it is. This book is filled with commonsense, instantly applicable ideas and tools that you can use to Make A Great Impression on the Customer (or anyone). To be MAGIC®.

Having over twenty-five years of experience in interpersonal training and consulting, we decided it was time to reach a broader audience and share our findings with the world. We are grateful that our publisher, Jossey-Bass, feels the same way. Our hope is that you will find the ideas useful and the stories inspiring.

Results matter, and so does the process used to get those results. In this book, we outline a logical process that yields tangible results. Making every contact MAGIC can be simple, and we guarantee you will stand out in the crowd if you apply these concepts in your daily business and personal interactions.

As you heighten your awareness of what the gold standard of customer service looks and feels like, you will see just how many little moments you have every day to make a difference. You will also become increasingly aware of how many hundreds of missed opportunities there were where you could have been treated better.

Our goal is to bring about a sea change so that the new norm is simply MAGIC. You will know when this is happening when you interact with like-minded people who are as excited about making your day better as you are about doing the same for them.

Have fun cleaning your restrooms. We'll see you there.

It really *is* that simple.

Westport, Connecticut   Diane Berenbaum
January 2007   Tom Larkin

How to Talk to Customers

PART ONE

The Essence of MAGIC

Five **MAGIC**, Memorable Minutes

"We met in a hotel lobby in Tulsa, Oklahoma. I was in town for the funeral of a dear family member. Gus was new at the hotel, but brought years of experience to his job at the front door. He had checked luggage at American Airlines for over thirty years.

"As I sat waiting for other family members to come downstairs that morning, I watched Gus in action—his gentle greeting, his outstretched hand; all were being welcomed in as family.

"Soon after that, I looked up to discover his hand was stretched my way with the same warm welcome I'd seen over and over again. Where the lobby had been bustling with ins and outs earlier, now all was quiet. He lingered, and we began to talk of life and family, and how much he loved his job. Soon my husband arrived. As we prepared to leave, Gus asked if he could follow along with our bags.

"He continued to visit with us. His gentle words were a warm blanket around my heart, as I admitted to myself that I had been wrestling with the events of the day. By the time we reached the car, my concerns about my family and the days ahead had lifted.

"Gus loaded our luggage into the car, then turned to me and said, 'Now I'm going to tuck you into your car and thank you for our time together this morning.'

"As we drove off, he bowed, and I felt comforted by his presence. If only he knew how he had blessed me that morning. Perhaps he does."

Isn't this the way customer service is supposed to be? Isn't this the type of interaction you wish you had every day? Yet the problem of poor customer service only seems to get worse.

Every once in a while, however, we as consumers have a truly wonderful experience as a customer of a company. These interactions leave us feeling so positive about our purchase, our relationships with the company, and ourselves that we say, "The experience was magic!" From LL Bean to American Century Investments to Nordstrom, there are a select few organizations—some you have heard of and some you haven't—that serve their customers at world-class levels day in and day out.

Although our opening story describes no more than five short minutes in one woman's life, those five minutes were certainly memorable. They were, indeed, MAGIC. (Throughout this book we will use the word "MAGIC" to describe any contact that "Makes A Great Impression on the Customer"—it's also the name of our customer service training program.)

Unfortunately, in many customer service interactions, five minutes can just as easily turn "tragic" instead. To illustrate this, we'll share the story of another colleague of ours.

Five **Tragic**, Memorable Minutes

"I recently had a very unfortunate phone call. I had discovered that I was not receiving certain e-mails.

"My conversation with the computer help desk person was like a 'Who's on first?' routine. First, he tested my computer and told me it was fine. No problems whatsoever. I told him that I knew of at least two e-mails that I had not received, and I was concerned that there were more. As I sent e-mails to myself, I received about nine out of ten. He sent me two, which I received, so he said all was well. I was not convinced.

"As a way to solve the problem, he wanted me to *send him all of the e-mails I had never received.* I'm not kidding! He needed to know when they were sent and how large they were. I tried to explain that I could not forward nor provide detailed info on e-mails that I never received. But he never understood.

"He never solved the problem. Later, I figured out that I had my e-mail open on another computer in the house, and it would download e-mail automatically every fifteen minutes or so. Those e-mails were counted as 'delivered,' so they never showed up in the e-mail box of my primary computer.

"No matter—thanks to that phone call, my frustration level was through the roof."

Everyone knows what it feels like to be in the shoes of our second colleague. You want to scream (and sometimes you do)! After those five tragic minutes that our colleague spent on the phone, she felt angry and frustrated—and certainly not likely to call technical support again. In contrast, the five MAGIC minutes described in our first story created a warm, pleasant memory that will be not only remembered for quite some time but retold again and again. Interactions like these, as short as they may be, can have a surprisingly strong personal impact, and they often affect how you feel for hours, days, and even months after they occur.

EFFECTIVE, MAGIC COMMUNICATION

Experiences such as these happen to all of us every day. It is exceedingly important to recognize both types of interactions and their effects. They represent two ever-present, distinct possibilities.

The disparity between those two possibilities carries far-reaching ramifications well beyond customer service interactions and into your personal, everyday life. How you communicate is the most dominant factor in your relationships with others—and, in turn, in the satisfaction you derive from your career and personal life. Simply put, your communication affects how others see you. In that sense, effective communication is at the heart of your ability to create an impression that puts you—your career, your business, and who you are as a person—in the best possible light.

Being a truly gifted communicator doesn't come naturally to most of us. In fact, communicating effectively today might even be more of a challenge than it was in the past. Today, we are all forced to contend with e-mails, voice messaging, and a wash of technology that, despite its claims to help communication, often serves to muddy waters that are already sufficiently murky.

But effective communication is within everyone's reach. One of the first steps toward this goal is recognizing that communication means more than a set of skills that someone can learn and practice. Instead, it begins with a mind-set. The right mind-set reflects your implicit respect for everyone around you and a commitment to demonstrate that respect. A courteous mind-set not only can mean better communication skills with clients and customers but also leads to a happier, more fulfilling life away from work.

This book has been written to help you have happier and more productive conversations with customers, on the telephone and in other business situations. MAGIC provides *the* gold standard of behavior that will motivate the people in your organization, delight your customers, and improve business results. However, the principles and power embodied by MAGIC are there to serve everyone, from corporate executives addressing an auditorium of shareholders, to two neighbors chatting over a picket fence.

HOW TO USE THIS BOOK

How you use this book is entirely up to you. Naturally, we hope you read it in its entirety, and we suggest you read it in order. Understanding the book as a whole is critical to embracing the concepts of MAGIC and, from there, putting them into everyday practice. However, you may be confronting a particular communication issue in either your business or your personal life. If that's the case, you may wish to pay particular attention to the part of the book most directly related to your area of interest.

In every chapter, you will find

- MAGIC and Tragic Moments
- Experiment with MAGIC
- MAGIC Maxims

MAGIC and Tragic Moments

MAGIC and Tragic Moments are real-life illustrations from customers, colleagues, and friends, and depict the various types of communication challenges we all face. We will explore each of these examples and demonstrate how you can address these challenges simply and effectively. They may make you smile or laugh, and they will perhaps trigger some of your own pleasant and not-so-pleasant memories of moments past.

Experiment with MAGIC

For this book to truly function as a learning tool, helping you reach your goal of becoming a more effective communicator, you will need to practice the skills we describe. The Experiment with MAGIC sections describe exercises that will help you better grasp MAGIC concepts and apply your new skills to your own daily interactions—personal and professional.

MAGIC Maxims

At the end of every chapter, we include a special feature we call MAGIC Maxims, a concise summary of the major ideas addressed in that particular chapter. They're an effective way to refresh your memory about the MAGIC concepts presented, as well as a way to think about how you might apply them.

Ultimately, we hope this book will do more than help you gain just one or two new skills, but instead will lead you to adopt a new way of thinking, a new mind-set. Think of this book as a learning tool and coach for improving your daily business and personal interactions. Use the exercises. Review the maxims. Empathize with the characters in the stories. By doing so, you will be well on your way to improving your communications and creating MAGIC moments in all your relationships.

What Does MAGIC Really Mean?

U p to this point, we've used the term MAGIC to describe a truly positive and memorable customer experience. And, to a certain extent, we've hinted at what that term implies. Now we'll move on to the details.

MAGIC is an acronym for **M**ake **A** **G**reat **I**mpression on the **C**ustomer. This is a straightforward concept; everyone in business wants to interact positively with customers and clients. You want them to feel good about what you do and how you do it. You want that feeling to be so persuasively positive that the thought of doing business with you again isn't even a debatable point—of course they're going to come back!

The same is true of your personal life. If you enjoy someone's company, you're naturally going to want to extend that relationship into the future.

But MAGIC is about more than just positive interactions. It is also about managing perception. It's been said that beauty is in the eye of the beholder, and nowhere is that more applicable than in your communications with others. The quality of your communication—be it with customers, friends, or family members—is really measured by how others perceive you.

You must make a choice—the choice to manage that perception, create a "quality" interaction, and make a great impression on the other person. Once you have made that choice, positive behavior follows.

MAKING THE CHOICE TO BE MAGIC

The importance of choice is the first central concept of MAGIC—one that you will see repeated as you proceed through the material. Perhaps the best way to illustrate the power of choice is to start off with a short anecdote:

> It was four days before Christmas, and I had a minor emergency. I backed my car into a rock and needed the car fixed right away. My insurance company was of little help, and they were anything but empathic. I found a local mechanic, Bill, with whom I had no previous experience.
>
> Not only did he repair my car, erasing all the remnants of the rock, but he personally delivered it to my front door on Christmas Eve. Here's the clincher: I hadn't even asked him to do so. As if he thought nothing of it, he simply said, "I didn't want you to be without your car for the holiday; and I know you have guests, so I brought your car to you."
>
> Bill's demonstration of exceptional service and regard for me as a person is the essence of respect and accountability that warms my heart. I can say, without reservation, that the next time my car breaks down I will not do business with anyone else but Bill.

In this story, Bill did everything he was supposed to do. He fixed the customer's car, and he did an excellent job of it. It's very likely that the customer would use Bill's services again even if he had done nothing more. However, because Bill made the choice to go the extra mile—outside of his job description—and relate personally to the customer, there is no doubt that when this customer's car breaks down again, he will bring it straight to Bill. Bill is a perfect example of someone choosing to be MAGIC.

The principle of choice applies to more than just choosing to go above and beyond what is expected. Choice is at the heart of effective communication, particularly in challenging or awkward circumstances. People at work often must take control of a negative situation and choose to turn it around. Instead of accepting style differences or misunderstandings as insurmountable, you can make a choice to improve the situation. You choose how to respond: to get angry or to listen and empathize before you respond.

For example, let's say that a customer is upset about something. He doesn't like your response, so he becomes angry and lashes out at you. Here's where choice comes into play. You can fuel the fire of his anger by responding in kind. Or, making a different choice, you can look past his seemingly irrational behavior and focus on helping him. In order to improve the situation, you choose to really listen to him and empathize with what's behind his emotion.

Many people are ineffective communicators because they choose to believe that there's simply no viable alternative. In this book, we'll show that there are more choices available, regardless of the situation.

COMMUNICATING WITH THE CUSTOMER IN MIND

Another aspect of the MAGIC mind-set is to relate to people in a way that is respectful and accountable. You never distort or sugarcoat the truth when talking to customers, but you keep your focus on the goal at hand: bringing the customer closer to a solution.

When you communicate with the customer in mind, you take a collaborative approach instead of sending an "us versus them" message. People who use a confrontational approach are more prone to quote policies, procedures, and the "company line" when it proves expedient to do so. You've undoubtedly heard the signs of the us-versus-them approach before:

"That's not the way we do things here!"

"You should have followed the directions!"

"Why did you do *that?!?*"

"If you had filled the form out right in the first place, you wouldn't have this problem."

"We didn't make a mistake—you did!"

After all, if you see yourself on one side of the fence and the customer on the other, it's awfully tempting to say almost anything to get her off the phone. You feel no sense of obligation to do otherwise.

To move beyond us-versus-them thinking, you need to remain open and receptive in every interaction, no matter how frustrating. Setbacks are completely understandable, and some are unavoidable. However, to avoid unnecessary upset, you must get in touch with your "hot buttons"—those customer responses that drive you crazy and trigger an emotional response. Some people react strongly when they hear emotion-driven accusations, such as "Don't you people know what you're doing?" or "You made a mistake on my statement again!"

MAGIC is about framing communication in the context of community, with a strong sense of relationship and connection between you and the customer. With commitment and practice, you'll find yourself choosing better responses naturally.

PRACTICAL TO THE UTMOST

A third aspect of MAGIC is its practical value. "Feeling good" isn't the only result of good communication; your business benefits when customers can express their needs to you and you can meet their needs. Any interaction, no matter how small, can be transformed from something ordinary to a memorable exchange that creates satisfaction and loyalty.

Let's say you're on the phone with a customer who is quite frustrated about receiving an inaccurate order. You acknowledge his experience of the situation—his frustrations. Then, working in concert, you address the problem quickly and efficiently. Your customer is relieved that you understood and that you "got" his frustration, and is pleased that the right order is now in the pipeline. And you're happy that the customer is genuinely satisfied.

Is that the end of the story? Not likely. By establishing a MAGIC relationship with a customer, you've cemented a connection that will influence that customer's choices in the future, just as Bill the mechanic did in the story at the beginning of this chapter. What customer wouldn't want to deal with a person or company whose every action reflects a commitment to service and integrity?

A **Tragic** Moment

Let's take a firsthand look at how your choices can affect the customer's experience and decision to do business with you again in the future.

"I went to a fancy frozen yogurt store in an upscale Boston mall that I passed through every day on my way to and from work. My mouth was watering for a certain chocolate flavor in the case. But the young lady behind the counter said, 'No, you can't have that. What else do you want?' She gave no explanation as to why she wouldn't give me the flavor I wanted. However, after some probing from me, she admitted it was too hard for her to scoop out. I then suggested she try running the scoop under hot water in the back of the store and then try again. She did that with a look on her face and, in the most perfunctory manner, made one quick attempt to scoop the chocolate and gave up. She said, 'No, can't do it. What else do you want?' As a final attempt (because I really wanted that chocolate), I suggested she put the container on the counter to soften up a bit. She refused and asked for the third time, 'What else do you want?' It didn't matter to her that I was a frequent customer.

"I walked out with nothing, but decided to return the next day to see if anyone else would help me. Fortunately for me, a young man was on duty. I told him what had happened the day before. He said, 'Ma'am, I'm not leaving until I get you that yogurt!' and immediately got it for me. However, he offered no apology and did not compensate me with extra yogurt or offer it free. Nevertheless, I would go back again simply because he said he would talk to the young lady who had annoyed me so much. Who knows if he ever did, but the thought that he might set her straight comforted me as a customer."

MAGIC **Maxims**

- MAGIC emphasizes relationships—not an us-versus-them attitude.
- MAGIC encourages self-awareness and learning so that you always put forth your personal best.
- MAGIC is not about sugarcoating or being nice for niceness's sake. It is about adopting a mind-set and gaining the skills necessary to interact effectively with others.
- MAGIC empowers you with choice. You can choose to be MAGIC or tragic in any situation—it's up to you.

chapter TWO

What Are the Benefits of MAGIC?

A **MAGIC** Moment

Our approach can help you prepare for any sort of challenge—even long-standing ones, like the situation a customer of ours encountered:

"I had an inspection this morning with a homeowner who has been a challenge for me in the past. When I pulled up to the home and realized who I was going to meet, I knew I could handle the situation.

"I took a deep breath, reminding myself to use MAGIC. The homeowner opened the door and had a look on her face that was priceless—almost a look of devil horns coming out of her head and steam coming from her ears.

"Despite her scary appearance, I had the confidence to take the next step with her. I greeted her with a smile and let her vent. Then I empathized and told her I was there to help. In about thirty seconds she turned into the wife from *Leave It to Beaver*. She looked relieved, and smiled. I addressed her issues and we came to an agreement, even though some things were not covered under our warranty policy. We set a deadline for her service, and she asked me if I would like a cup of coffee for the road. Wow! What typically is at least one to one-and-a-half hours with her was dropped to just twenty minutes because I approached it with a totally different attitude."

Let's take the idea of having a personal sense of self-confidence a few steps further. As we pointed out earlier, people have choices in how they behave and respond to others.

When members of an organization individually and collectively make the choice to forge connections, they create what we like to refer to as a "MAGIC culture"—a professional environment where people treat one another with just as much respect and sense of community as they do a customer on the other end of the telephone. In this way, a culture is built and nurtured from the inside out—having a positive impact on everyone who may come in contact with that environment.

Just think of what such a culture can do for your business. Imagine a team of committed, enthusiastic employees who bring their "A-game" to every element of their work responsibility—and, thanks to a supportive and nurturing work environment, stay and grow alongside your business. A team like that can generate some very impressive numbers! (More about the culture of MAGIC in Chapter Seventeen.)

CARING CREATES PROFITS

A few years back, a survey conducted by the Rockefeller Corporation of Pittsburgh queried some 450 executives from a variety of businesses and industrial fields. They were asked to identify the most common reasons why a customer stopped doing business with them—why, in other words, a client or customer suddenly pulled up stakes and chose another company with which to do business.

Before reading further, grab a piece of paper and take a few minutes to write down what you think might have been on that rather unfortunate grouping.

Here's the list, in all its infamy:

- Death—1 percent
- A move or relocation—2 percent
- A relationship with a salesperson—4 percent
- Price and other relevant costs—11 percent
- Dissatisfaction with the product—14 percent
- Attitude of indifference from someone representing the company—68 percent

Surprised by that last figure? Many people are just about dumbstruck by this revelation, but these are the facts in black and white. Amid everything else that can go wrong—either by sheer happenstance or someone's miscalculation or mistake—

nearly seven out of ten highly placed businesspeople identified indifference as the primary push that shoves a customer out the door.

An employee who is nasty with a customer is not indifferent, nor is a telephone rep who provides inaccurate or out-of-date information or guidance.

Indifference refers to a perceived lack of interest or attention to the customer, client, or caller. If you think about it, being rude or making a mistake, at the very least, requires some sort of effort. Indifference doesn't even have that going for it! Instead, it's like an apathetic shell—a cocoon that an employee can crawl into when anything approaching bona fide effort or interest just doesn't seem to be worth it.

In fact, the problem can be even more insidious in that an employee may not even know that he is coming across as indifferent. This is not surprising—it's easy to think that one is a consummate professional because one has had years of experience. But a customer may see an employee in a totally different light because of the way she comes across on the telephone. It's the customer's perception that counts. Customers can make a decision about you, your department, and your company from just one contact. All it takes is one drab "How may I help you?"—which, in effect, suggests "How may I *not* help you?"—to send a signal of indifference. And, worse, send that customer to a competitor.

A **Tragic** Moment

One of our facilitators shared a story about being treated with indifference:

"I was in Wisconsin on business and, having forgotten my toothpaste, visited the local drug store. I found my product and went to check out. When I arrived at the register, the cashier completely ignored me. She grabbed my toothpaste, robotically scanned it, then thrust out her hand as if to say, "Just give me the money, wouldya?" I handed her the money, and she gave me my change, still without acknowledging me in any way.

"At that instant I realized that this person had not said one word to me. During that quick moment I also looked at her name tag. You will never guess what it said: 'Cashier of the Month.' I was horrified by the thought of what the other cashiers might be like. I quickly walked away thinking I would never return to that store."

It's easy to imagine just how harmful an attitude of indifference can be to clients and customers. If you need additional evidence, consider this recent research from Technical Assistance Research Programs Inc. (TARP), for more than thirty years a specialist and innovator in the measurement and management of customer loyalty. According to TARP, it costs five times as much to obtain a new customer as it does to retain an existing one through superior contact handling. Depending on the industry, that ratio can actually run as high as twenty to one (*Basic Facts on Customer Complaint Behavior and the Impact of Service on the Bottom Line.* Arlington, Va.: TARP Worldwide U.S., 1999, p. 3).

Think about it: it's not particularly expensive for an employee to do what he can to keep an existing customer as happy as possible. A bit of time, a bit of effort, certainly, but by no means back breaking. But identify just some of the steps—and the expense involved—of luring a new customer into the fold: the cost of marketing materials and product information, the salary of the sales reps who call on prospects, the time expended to set up an account and answer the wash of inevitable questions that any new customer is likely to have.

More facts add to the case:

- Personal interaction over the phone can have twenty times the impact of ads in terms of shaping customer opinion and generating referrals, according to TARP.

- Nearly two-thirds of customers in a Benchmark Portal study said they would stop using a company if they had one bad experience (Purdue University. "How Did the Telephone Agent Do in Satisfying Your Needs and Handling Your Call?" Benchmark Portal, www.benchmarkportal.com/newsite/article_detail.taf?topicid=276 [accessed Oct. 19, 2006]). And 49 percent said their experience with a company was "very important" in shaping their image of that company (Purdue University. "Do You Feel Call Experience Is Important in Shaping the Image of the Company?" Benchmark Portal, www.benchmark-portal.com/newsite/article_detail.taf?topicid=283 [accessed Oct. 19, 2006]).

That's why, from a business standpoint, it's imperative to create the best impression and head off the catastrophic destruction that indifference can bring.

CUT CUSTOMER LOSS, BOOST YOUR BOTTOM LINE

Even a small reduction in customer defections can have enormous benefits. To illustrate: the *Harvard Business Review* reports that companies that reduce customer loss by 5 percent can, as a result, boost profits by as much as 85 percent ("Zero Defections: Quality Comes to Service," Sept.-Oct. 1990, pp. 103-111). That's some payback. Trim customer defections even more and watch your earnings soar.

Other empirical data also support the importance of solid customer service. Consider, if you will, these additional numbers provided by TARP: businesses with a consistent level of high-quality service gain market share at a rate of 6 percent a year and can charge approximately 10 percent more than competitors.

These data show how businesses with an established benchmark of high-quality service earn a more prominent role in their marketplaces. But particularly provocative is the idea that customers are ready and willing to pay more for service that they expect to be top drawer.

Put it all together, and the practical benefits of MAGIC speak for themselves:

- Customers who stay on board with your company

- Customers who genuinely value the experience they have with your company

- Customers who happily pay a premium for a high-quality service experience

Here are just some of the measurable results reported by companies who have embraced MAGIC:

- The Alger Fund achieved the most prestigious award for service quality in the mutual fund industry.

- Aston Martin Jaguar Land Rover North America, a division of Ford Motor Company, showed significant improvement in courteousness, professionalism, willingness to listen, and commitment to help.

- DST Systems improved their customer satisfaction ratings and moved from the bottom to the top quartile.

- UnumProvident reported the highest courtesy score ever in their history—98 percent.

- Evenflo Company noted that their culture changed and that employees are more helpful and willing to assist callers regardless of the situation.

In Part Two, we'll begin to discuss how to build that very special sort of environment.

MAGIC **Maxims**

- Just as beauty is in the eye of the beholder, indifference is in the eye of the customer.

- Perceived indifference is by far the leading cause of customer defections.

- High-quality service such as that fostered by MAGIC means increased customer referrals and greater market share.

- Customers willingly pay more for great service.

PART TWO

MAGIC—
It's Your Choice

chapter THREE

Releasing Your MAGIC Mind-Set

What do we mean when we refer to the MAGIC mind-set? It's a belief in people and in the indisputable power of serving others. We're not talking about a power *over* people. We're really talking about the effect you can have on others through your way of relating or responding to them. How you do this comes down to choice—a choice that's within you and one you make from moment to moment.

THE MAGIC IS WITHIN YOU

We have countless stories of colleagues and friends who have released the MAGIC within them on a regular basis—both in their professional lives as well as in other settings. You'll see their stories in our MAGIC Moments as you read on.

MAGIC works, time and time again. It makes your business better and more profitable, it makes your work environment more pleasant and constructive, and it can make every one of your relationships more enjoyable and rewarding.

Ever notice how, in certain instances, you find just the right words, and your customer (or friend or relative, for that matter) responds in a way that's so much better than you expected? On other days, you may respond in a reactive way that produces a less desirable result. In this book, we identify those behaviors that make a positive difference so that you become aware of what they are—and can use them every day.

A **MAGIC** Moment

MAGIC is inside everyone. If you doubt it, perhaps a story from a friend of ours may change your mind.

"I had to go to the DMV one day to get a new license plate. After thirty minutes of waiting, my number finally came up. It was obvious that the person behind the counter wasn't in particularly great spirits. She looked down and just barked orders to me. I forgot to sign one of the forms, and she scolded me, tossing it back in my direction. Throughout the whole thing, I was determined to remain calm, so I did—I even smiled when she chastised me for forgetting to sign my name.

"When we were done, she grabbed a plate at random and, again, tossed it to me. I couldn't believe my eyes when I saw the plate: 123-DOG. Everyone knows how much I love dogs, so, even though it was chosen entirely at random, it was just perfect.

"I couldn't help myself. 'Thank you!' I gushed. 'I love it! You've made my day.' From there, her entire demeanor was transformed. She started smiling—she started treating me like a friend, chatting and laughing. As I left, she even went so far as to say what a pleasure it was to have helped me and how glad she was that I liked the plate.

"Then it dawned on me. The way I treated her affected how she responded to me. I realized then that MAGIC is truly within everyone."

CREATE THE RIGHT ENVIRONMENT

Wherever you are, wherever you go, you can create the ideal environment for communication, one that creates a positive experience for you and others around you.

If you know you have the skills to work with others effectively, your attitude toward them is going to reflect that—you know you're ready to address whatever may warrant your attention. You are less likely to have your back up or be defensive. You are also less likely to be overly cautious, holding back. Instead, you're confident and willing to engage.

In essence, choosing a MAGIC mind-set will influence your behavior—in all sorts of ways. The tone of your voice (an important element we'll talk about later) will be positive and engaging. Your listening skills (yet another critical ingredient) will be sharpened and at the ready. Although in a telephone conversation your body language won't be visible to the other person, it will nonetheless manifest itself in the way you come across. And, of course, if you are in a face-to-face setting, your body language will reflect the positive words you use in the conversation.

When you consistently express this mind-set, you will influence others' behavior. They'll respond in a different way than they otherwise might, creating a positive environment for all.

Experiment with MAGIC

Try this exercise the next time you're on the phone—particularly if you're dealing with a difficult or challenging call. No matter the circumstances or the words you happen to choose for your remarks, smile. That's right, keep smiling no matter what. As you do so, pay attention to how you sound, the tone of what you say—not to mention the words and phrases you happen to choose. You may be surprised to discover that your facial expression is not simply a matter of cosmetics; a smile actually can have a direct influence on the way you interact with others.

Much of what we are describing comes back to the importance of choice—not only in your decision to work with a customer, no matter how difficult she may be, but in your conscious choice of attitude, the mind-set you bring to that interaction. With MAGIC, you make the choice to respect the other person and treat her as you would have her treat you; your attitude and behavior naturally reflect that commitment.

This also applies to personal relationships. In many ways, family, friends, and coworkers are, in fact, "customers." They have an investment in a relationship with you.

The bottom line: MAGIC helps you establish a genuinely respectful relationship between you and others, and enables you to

- Understand that every person you communicate with is your "customer."

- Recognize that every communication makes an impression—everything counts!

- Realize that every contact can be handled so appropriately that the "customer" naturally chooses to have further contact with you—even if you deliver bad news.

That's right: even if you have to tell the customer that his product was back-ordered or that his ID card isn't ready—or must say no in any fashion—he can still feel that you've handled the call in such a calm, confident, professional way that he would choose to have another contact with you in the future.

THE CUSTOMER IS ALWAYS . . . WHAT?

Everyone under the sun knows the one business mantra that supposedly takes supreme precedence over all others: "The customer is always right."

Wrong, pure and simple. The customer isn't always right. But the customer is, in the end, still the customer.

That is a huge difference. Consider this scenario: a customer buys a bread knife and then promptly breaks it when, in the throes of some late-night infomercial delusion, tries to saw his way through a brick retaining wall. He returns with the knife, admits that he misused it, then begins to shout at the customer service rep who, understandably enough, is hesitant to refund money to someone who used the product as inappropriately as he possibly could have.

Is this customer—one whose lack of common sense is equaled only by his predilection for verbal abuse—*right?* Not in the universe most of us inhabit. But, despite his bizarre behavior, he is still the customer.

Is the customer ever wrong? Do customers make mistakes when using a product, or incorrectly recall a feature of a warranty? We've all been customers, and we can all admit that we've been wrong at some point!

So what's the real issue underlying the misguided "The customer's always right" adage? When you think about it, who is right or wrong is beside the point. The critical issue is one of treating everyone as valuable. Customers are valuable; they provide insights into the use of your product and how to improve it. Employees likewise are valuable. When companies and organizations build fences based on right and wrong, they can only breed win-lose scenarios.

What does all this mean? It means that a customer—no matter how unpleasant or irrational—is still due the respect and attention that the most courteous customer would warrant. It also means that he deserves the utmost integrity in the way in which you interact with him.

What it does *not* mean is giving the customer carte blanche to be abusive—or, for that matter, to automatically expect every little detail to go just the way he wants.

In that sense, your goal is to establish a constructive middle ground between you and the customer. In one respect, you're prepared to do whatever is reasonable to help. At the same time, however, the customer doesn't have license to run roughshod over you in the process or to bully her way into getting everything she wants. The principle of mutual respect and value is paramount. And for situations where mutuality is lacking, we'll share some valuable self-preservation skills to get you through.

A **MAGIC** Moment

A rep fielded a call from a prominent radio personality who was experiencing difficulty with his vehicle and was extremely upset. Here's what she told us:

"A customer called me on Friday. . . . He was very upset, to the point where I had to pull the phone away from my ear. He said, 'I want to end my lease *now.* If you don't let me do that, I will tell my million listeners to never buy a car from your company!'"

"This was the most irate person I've ever spoken with. And I completely turned him around using MAGIC. First, I connected with him by using his name and empathizing. I said, 'Mr. Hudson, I see that you have really had it with our company. My name is Sylvia, and I am here to help you. Please tell me what happened.' Well, after that, he told me the whole story. I just listened and told him that I understood what he was going through. Then I did everything I could to help him. He's now my best friend. In fact, I'm sitting here looking at a beautiful bouquet of flowers he sent to me. He actually purchased a $90,000 sports car from our company as a result of my conversation with him! It was really an incredible turnaround. I couldn't have done it without MAGIC."

MAGIC **Maxims**

- Every person you communicate with is your customer—every day and everywhere!

- Every communication, no matter how brief or seemingly insignificant, makes an impression.

- The goal of MAGIC is to handle every contact so appropriately that the customer chooses to have another contact with you again—even if you delivered bad news.

- The customer is not always right—but the customer is still the customer and has value.

chapter FOUR

Create a Climate for MAGIC Relationships

Now we get down to the heart of the discussion: concrete steps for establishing a positive and constructive environment for communication.

It all starts with your choice to control your side of any relationship—how you respond to clients, customers, coworkers, and anyone else with whom you interact. By controlling your side of a relationship, you can also influence the overall environment in which that relationship takes place.

THERMOSTATS AND THERMOMETERS

Consider the purpose of a thermostat for a moment. Its function is to establish the temperature within a particular room or space. Crank it up, and the room gets hot enough to bake muffins. Drop it down low enough, and you're making small talk with a polar bear.

In other words, a thermostat has a powerful impact on the environment that surrounds it.

Now consider the thermostat as a metaphor for yourself as a communicator. How you interact with others is, effectively, a thermostat—a device that establishes a tone for your environment and the atmosphere with the people with whom you may be talking. Like a thermostat that defines the environment in a physical space, your communication "thermostat" sets the stage for your communication environment.

Now think of another image: a thermometer. True, it's like a thermostat in that its function relates to the temperature, but that's where any similarity ends. A thermostat sets the temperature; a thermometer reacts to the temperature and merely reads what's already there.

So ask yourself this question: Do you see yourself as a thermostat or a thermometer? As we've pointed out earlier, MAGIC communication is about taking the lead in setting the tone of your communication with others. It's not a question of who speaks first. It's a question of attitude. It is the words you choose and other elements, but it boils down to a desire and ability to manage the impression that you convey to others. Communication is not merely a means of reaction.

If you are in fact a thermostat, what kind of communication climate are you establishing? Sure, you may be taking the lead and setting the tone rather than merely reacting, but what sort of environment are you putting in place? Is it positive and constructive or hostile and indifferent?

If you wish to establish a communication setting where a customer has a positive experience—and, as a result, is prompted to want to return—it's essential that you act as a thermostat to establish a positive, constructive environment, no matter what anyone else may happen to bring to the table. Put another way, you can choose the setting of the thermostat that sets the climate around you.

The setting of that thermostat matters all the time, without fail. That's because every time you talk with someone, you make some sort of impression. It may be positive, neutral, or negative, but you make one nonetheless. And those impressions add up over time.

A **MAGIC** Moment

A friend of ours does a terrific job of explaining how important climate is in almost any setting:

"Tanya is the most MAGIC teller I have ever met. She works at the bank across the street from my office. She is always friendly, helpful, and efficient—clearly she knows what she's doing. I can't say that is true about anyone else who works there. They seem to just go through the motions. Whenever I call the bank, I ask to speak with Tanya; I really don't want to talk with anyone else. I perk up when I hear her cheery voice. We've gotten to know each other, and it's a great relationship.

"One day when I went into the bank, I stood in line and hoped that I would get to speak with Tanya. Then I noticed an unusual thing. People ahead of me in line were letting others go in front of them so they could speak with Tanya as well. She shines like no other bank representative I have ever known. I told her to tell me if and when she ever decides to leave this bank—I'll leave, too!"

FOCUS ON WHAT YOU CAN CONTROL

We've been talking a lot about choosing how you act and react. But let's not lose sight of a bit of obvious reality: not everything is within your control.

Experiment with MAGIC

Here's an exercise that will help you clarify the concept of control. Take a piece of paper and draw a line down the middle. At the top of the left-hand column write "Can control." Above the right, write "Can't control."

Take a few minutes—say, no more than five—to write down the things you can and cannot control in your workday. Keep it as practical and reasonable as possible.

Now review your lists. Notice the number of things that you consider beyond your control. Perhaps it is a longer list than what you have for "Can control" and may include such items as corporation-wide policies and procedures, legal regulations, what customers say, and your coworkers' actions. Things like this can make you feel overwhelmed and stressed out.

Now take a look at those things that you believe you can control. Some of the more obvious ones might be the quality of your work or how often you arrive at the office on time.

But there may be other items that are somewhat less obvious. See if any of the following come close to what you have down on your list:

- My attitude
- How I use my time

- What I say and how I say it

- How I respond to customers and colleagues

- How I manage my workload

- My knowledge

- What I can do if I see something wrong or inappropriate

As your lists show, there are some things that you simply cannot out-and-out control. But if you take a closer look at your "Can't control" side of the ledger, you might see that there are some things you can influence in a positive way.

For instance, you may not be able to control a corporation-wide policy with which you don't agree, but you may be able to offer feedback to someone with some influence over that policy. Your input may not change the policy completely, but it may lead to some sort of change.

Did you happen to have "how customers react" on your list of things you can't control? How about "the volume of calls" or "other departments"? Step back and ask yourself, "Is there any way that I can influence these things?" The answer is . . . absolutely!

How you interact with customers (and the words and tone you use) will most definitely influence customers' reactions. And if you work with customers in such a professional way that you resolve their issues in one call, you can influence the number of callbacks and complaint calls that come in. You can even increase the likelihood that other departments will do what they say they will do by modeling that behavior yourself.

This give-and-take between you and others and your environment can be described as your *locus of control*. If you were to apply a physical image to it, it might be one of a large circle. You're in the middle; everyone and everything else forms a ring around you. Two-way arrows between you and everything that surrounds you represent the give-and-take of interaction and influence. No matter the swirl of people, events, and influences around you, you can always control what you say, think, or do in any situation—if you choose to do so.

This is a wonderful, powerful choice to make. And if you have decided to make that choice, you're ready to move on to The Five MAGIC Steps.

A **MAGIC** Moment

An associate shared this story about the impact of choice:

"I recently visited the offices of a large insurance company. Walking past Fred's cube, I saw the computer screens go blank and noticed Fred tapping the computer urgently—Ctrl-Alt-Delete got some very assertive presses. Then with frustration and angst, Fred stood up and announced to the entire center, 'The system is down!' (How many people do you think needed that information?) After he slammed his headset on the desk, he said he would take a break.

"As I continued walking, I saw Sarah attempting the same keyboard solutions, to no avail. But her choices showed up in dramatic contrast. She slid her headset down, reached into her inbox, and began doing some paperwork.

"If you didn't know there was a system crash, you would not have known anything had interrupted Sarah's workday. Despite the system glitch, she effortlessly moved to other work that could be done.

"Sarah and Fred exhibited some very different choices. Sometimes the choices you make influence your productivity. I don't think the system crash distracted Sarah; she was too busy being productive."

MAGIC **Maxims**

- Consider yourself a thermostat that sets the tone for your relationships.
- Recognize what you can and cannot control.
- Recognize what you can influence—and what, in turn, influences you.
- Remember that you can always choose how you respond to any situation or circumstance.

PART THREE

Build MAGIC Relationships

First Steps

A n old saying goes, "You never get a second chance to make a first impression."

There's a good deal of truth to that. Granted, some of us are better than others at recovering from a less than auspicious start in a conversation or relationship. For many, however, it can be difficult or nearly impossible to reverse a first impression. Getting off on the right foot can make things so much easier and more pleasant from the very start.

This means that the first moments in any conversation are critical. They set the tone for what comes later. On top of that, they have a significant effect on both you and the person with whom you're talking. Not only do you want to come across in the best possible light—to be seen as professional, courteous, and ready to help—but doing so puts the other person at ease and readies her to participate in a constructive, enjoyable conversation.

Experiment with MAGIC

Take out a piece of paper and jot down everything you can think of that creates an impression—both on the telephone and in face-to-face encounters. Write every detail you can. You might want to think of a recent situation in which you were the customer—perhaps you called your cellular phone provider or paid a visit to your local bank. Consider everything that made an impression, from beginning to end.

If you're like most folks, you'll end up with a pretty full list, including such items as the person's tone of voice, choice of words, eye contact, knowledge, listening, courtesy, and overall attitude. This isn't surprising—many things contribute to the impression we have of others, perhaps a great deal more than we might realize.

GETTING TO KNOW THE FIVE MAGIC STEPS

As we mentioned earlier, MAGIC stands for Make A Great Impression on the Customer. But it is also our name for a collection of the best practices that help you reach that goal.

By "best practices" we mean the skills that represent the most effective service behaviors. To make these skills memorable, we refer to them as The 33 Points of MAGIC™. (We'll begin talking about these points in Chapter Fifteen.) The points in the overall list are grouped into five steps, each represented by a letter of the word *MAGIC* and each comprising specific behaviors designed to move the conversation forward. They are The Five MAGIC Steps:

M Make a Connection: Build the Relationship

A Act Professionally: Express Confidence

G Get to the Heart of the Matter: Listen and Ask Questions

I Inform and Clarify What You Will Do

C Close with the Relationship in Mind

At a glance, you can see how these five steps taken in turn unite to create an effective flow for an interaction. With the first step, you set the climate for a positive, professional conversation. From the start, the customer will feel comfortable with you and confident that you can help. From there, you ask questions and move the discussion toward the central issue and provide appropriate solutions. The call concludes with agreement and a constructive wrap-up.

With these in mind, let's start with the first step, Make a Connection: Build the Relationship.

MANAGING PERCEPTION

Refer back to your list of those things that create an impression. Do you notice that many of the items you wrote down relate to the person with whom you're speaking—specifically, his words, tone, and body language? These are indeed the core elements that make up an impression.

But there's more to them than meets the eye—literally. Dr. Albert Mehrabian, known for his pioneering work in psychology and communication, found that when there is inconsistency in the communication of attitude and feelings between verbal and nonverbal cues, people tend to believe the nonverbal (*Silent Messages: Implicit Communication of Emotions and Attitudes, Second Edition.* Belmont, Calif.: Wadsworth, 1981, p. 77). Here are his findings:

- 55 percent of the message of face-to-face communication comes through visual elements, such as facial expression and body language.
- 38 percent comes through tone of voice.
- 7 percent comes through the words themselves.

These numbers make sense. We've all been in situations where a company representative is saying all the "right" things, such as "My name is Shirley. I'd be happy to help you today. Let me know if you have any questions." Unfortunately, too often the message you get is quite the opposite of what the scripted words are intended to convey. Your real perception is that Shirley is indifferent—or worse.

How did you get that impression? Not from the words; they were saying all the right things. Most likely it was through nonverbal elements. An apathetic tone or minimal eye contact will contradict or even cancel out the most positive wording.

For the time being, let's concentrate on telephone conversations—where the visual element is removed from the equation. What's left? Words and tone. Given the results of Mehrabian's research, we can surmise that tone will have a far greater impact on perception than words.

Harkening back to our discussion of the importance of control earlier in this book, Mehrabian's findings highlight those two elements that are under your control when you begin a conversation: the words you use and, even more important, your tone of voice. They are within your locus of control. They're critical to creating the impression you want to convey and establishing a basis for a relationship with the caller.

MAKE A GREAT IMPRESSION FROM THE START

Let's go back to the acronym MAGIC. The first letter is M, which stands for Make a Connection. That's what you need to do at the start—establish a connection with the person at the other end of the line. The goal is to make him feel welcome, comfortable, and important.

A visual image is helpful here in identifying the sort of start you establish with any phone conversation. Think of a stoplight: red, yellow, and green. If you're driving, you know full well what they mean. Red is stop; yellow means proceed with caution; green tells you to go ahead.

The type of greeting you use at the beginning of a conversation functions exactly like that signal light. What sort of attitude and impression are you conveying? Are your tone and attitude upbeat and engaging? Or are you sending mixed signals through your words and tone?

Whether you realize it or not, your greetings send a signal to your customers. What kind have others sent to you?

Red light: You can instantly tell that the person on the phone doesn't want to help you at all. That's a stop signal. It's a complete turnoff because she speaks too fast, uses a monotone voice, or is simply curt.

Yellow light: This is a warning, cautionary signal. You get a sense that the representative may not be able or willing to help. Something in the tone or pace suggests that he's not fully present or ready to help.

Green light: This is the signal that the associate is ready, willing, and able to help. The words, tone, and pace let you know you have a professional on the other end of the line. You feel comfortable and secure as a result.

Experiment with MAGIC

As we've discussed, attitude and tone are absolutely central to starting off a conversation on the right foot. To gauge where you may be—and whether, in fact, your tone and attitude may benefit from a tune-up—try the following exercise.

Using a tape recorder or some other recording device, record the greeting you use when you pick up the telephone. Simple as that. Just say what you would say under the most normal of circumstances. For instance, if you work in customer support, it might be "Hi, this is Darlene in customer service. How can I help you?" Or, in sales, "Sales, this is Jim." Whatever it is, record it. Be absolutely honest: don't tinker with a greeting that you may think is subpar in some respects. Just record what you normally say.

Now play it back and listen to yourself. What do you hear? How would your greeting make you feel if you were the caller at the other end of the line? Do you sound upbeat, ready to help—in effect, happy that you're in a position to provide that person with service? Or do you come across some other way: bored, unhappy, or sounding as though the caller is somehow intruding on your valuable time?

This exercise can be very telling. By listening to yourself, you get a more accurate sense of the attitude and tone you routinely convey at the outset of a conversation—a sense of whether you're giving that caller a red, yellow, or green light. As we've discussed, the greeting is critical to making a great impression from the start.

Note: you can certainly do this exercise on your own and perform a self-evaluation of your tone and attitude. But let's face it: we tend to be rather forgiving of ourselves. So it's helpful to carry this out as a group exercise, with several people recording their greetings and offering each other their feedback. That way, you're likely to gain perspective and insight you may have missed if you rely solely on what you yourself happen to hear.

To further your understanding, use the list here to identify the message you're sending with your greeting. Circle the number that best represents your impression from each person's greeting.

Cheerful	1	2	3	4	5	6	7	Not cheerful at all
Good at his or her job	1	2	3	4	5	6	7	Poor at his or her job
Interested	1	2	3	4	5	6	7	Bored
Self-assured	1	2	3	4	5	6	7	Ill at ease
Educated	1	2	3	4	5	6	7	Uneducated
Trustworthy	1	2	3	4	5	6	7	Untrustworthy
Friendly	1	2	3	4	5	6	7	Unfriendly
Intelligent	1	2	3	4	5	6	7	Unintelligent
Enthusiastic	1	2	3	4	5	6	7	Apathetic
Impressive	1	2	3	4	5	6	7	Unimpressive
Polite	1	2	3	4	5	6	7	Impolite
Professional	1	2	3	4	5	6	7	Amateurish
Kind	1	2	3	4	5	6	7	Unkind
Mature	1	2	3	4	5	6	7	Immature
Pleasant	1	2	3	4	5	6	7	Unpleasant

Don't be discouraged if your "traffic light" is malfunctioning just a bit. The good news is that by hearing yourself and recognizing opportunities for improvement, you're well on your way to sending a green light every time.

THE WORDS YOU USE

If you simply grab the phone and say "Hello," it's awfully hard to come across positively no matter how much you may consciously concentrate on your tone. Let's focus on the words you choose and their impact.

1. **Welcoming words.** These phrases help you establish a connection. They may be used at the beginning or end of your greeting. The following are some examples:

"Good morning [afternoon]."

"Thank you for calling ABC Co."

"May I help you?"

"How may I help you today?"

These and other expressions like them help the customer feel welcome.

Note: we recommend that you not use welcoming words at the beginning and end of your greeting. This can make the greeting too long, which may cause you to rush through it. Just choose a phrase that is most comfortable for you.

2. **Location, location, location.** It's essential to let the caller know who she has contacted and where you happen to be. By mentioning the location, you are communicating with the customer in mind.

If you're taking an outside call, first say your company's name. It's important—callers want to know from the get-go that they've reached the place they want to call. On top of that, people often misdial numbers, and if by chance they get the wrong recipient, they appreciate knowing that from the outset. We've all called places where someone mumbles something incoherent, leading to an awkward silence before we ask, "Uh, is this Brown and Co.?" Avoid that scenario at all costs.

Consider telling the caller the department or specific area he has reached. This removes any doubt and helps him feel comfortable. To gauge whether your particular situation warrants providing this sort of specific information, just listen to your callers. If they're frequently confused or at a loss as to where they've ended up, a few more specifics certainly wouldn't hurt.

3. **The name game.** You have a choice: use either your full name or just your first. (Of course, your company's policy may have something to say about this.) Whichever your choice, using your name serves to personalize the call and place you and the caller on the same playing field. And chances are good that she'll tell you her name in return. In the absence of eye contact or a handshake over the phone, giving your name removes the anonymity factor and begins to establish relationship.

4. **Putting it all together.** Pick the combination of words that's most comfortable for you; just remember to use welcoming words at the beginning or end and your name and location. Here are some examples:

"Good morning, ABC Co. This is Mary Johnson."

"Thank you for calling Comprehensive Mortgage. This is Justin."

"Benefit Services Center. This is Ruth. How may I help you?"

If you know the caller is internal, then you can choose to eliminate the location:

"Good morning. This is Jim."

"This is Marguerite. May I help you?"

Exhibit 5.1 summarizes what we've just discussed.

Exhibit 5.1: Your Greeting

"Good morning" ["Good afternoon"]* or "Thank you for calling"*	Company or department name	Your name	"May I help you?"*

Note: * Choose just one of these welcoming phrases.

Experiment with MAGIC

Each of the following greetings needs a makeover. What would you do to make them MAGIC?

1. "General Insurance, this is Lindsay speaking."

2. "HR, may I help you?"

3. "Friendly Insurance, this is Peter. May I have your identification number, please?"

4. "XYZ Carpet. Marty Jones here. Can I help you?"

Learn why these greetings are "tragic" and find MAGIC makeovers near the end of the chapter.

TONE AND PACE

Even the most thoughtfully chosen words—made up of the elements discussed in the prior section—are of little value if you speak in a bored, weary voice or a monotone that sends a message that you just don't care.

By the same token, don't overdo it. Don't sound so overenthusiastic that the caller wonders how much caffeine may be surging through your veins. Also watch the balance of your tone—avoid going up and down too much or sounding as though you're singing the words. That can sound canned and insincere. If you maintain an upbeat tone throughout your greeting, you'll send a message that you care and truly want to help.

Another key element is pace. On the one hand, you don't want to speak so slowly that it sounds as though ether is being pumped into your office. But watch out for too fast a pace. If you speak too quickly, your words can become muddied, and, worse, you can lose those valuable inflections in your tone that express sincerity and a willingness to help. You can also come across as being in a rush and hoping to get through the conversation as quickly as possible (implying that you have more important things to do). No customer likes to be rushed or to feel as though he were an imposition.

Finally, if you speak too fast, your customer may not catch your message and will begin to wonder if she's called the right place. You may then have to repeat the information again, which starts you off on the wrong foot and lengthens the call.

A **Tragic** Moment

Sometimes people don't realize the impact of the first words they say. See how one of our associates was put off by a receptionist's greeting:

"I called our law firm and asked if a specific lawyer was available. The receptionist's response was, 'I don't know. I'm not on his floor.'

"I then asked to be transferred to him.

"His secretary answered the phone and sounded somewhat annoyed—as though I had made her pick up the phone. I gave my name and asked if our lawyer was available. Her response was, 'Who's this?' I told her my name. Her response: 'Are you a client?' I told her that I had worked with this firm for the last twelve years. Once she knew I was a client, she became very friendly. I wonder what she would have said if I had said I was not a client!"

Clearly, the management of this firm has not thought about the impressions its employees make on incoming callers.

MAGIC **Makeovers**

Remember those tragic greetings we looked at earlier? Let's take a look at why they are tragic, and how you can make them MAGIC.

1. *"General Insurance, this is Lindsay speaking."*

   What makes this greeting tragic?

   - There are no welcoming words. It would send a more positive signal if it started with "Good morning [good afternoon]" or ended with "May I help you?"

   - "Lindsay speaking." Although this phrase is commonly heard, it is routine—and confusing. Why? Two reasons: (1) it hides Lindsay's name, and it can sound as if "speaking" is Lindsay's last name; (2) it's obvious that she's speaking! It would come across as clearer and more professional if she were to say, "This is Lindsay."

2. *"HR, may I help you?"*

This greeting is anonymous. Add your name after the department, and you're all set.

3. *"Friendly Insurance, this is Peter. May I have your identification number please?"*

Although there is an attempt at using welcoming words, the greeting becomes cold and impersonal with the request for an ID number. It sends a signal that the caller is just a number rather than a customer with a question or need.

Just tweak that final phrase by using a "May I help you?" instead.

4. *"XYZ Carpet. Marty Jones here. Can I help you?"*

For a couple of reasons, this greeting is not as professional as it could be. First, "Marty Jones here" sounds casual, a little sloppy. After all, you're representing a place of work. Instead, use "This is Marty Jones" to send a more polished message.

Second, the word "can" puts one's ability in question. It could prompt a response like "I don't know—can you?" The word "may" relates to permission; it is a gracious way to engage a customer. So ending the greeting with "May I help you?" makes a more professional impression.

MAGIC **Maxims**

- Remember that customers form an impression of you and your company from your words, tone, and body language.

- Don't underestimate the importance of your greeting. Like a handshake, it makes a lasting impression.

- Use welcoming words, such as "Good morning" or "Thank you for calling," at the beginning or end of your greeting.

- Be sure your tone is upbeat so that the customer gets the message that you care and are ready to help.

- Watch the pace of your greeting. Too slow can suggest boredom; too fast may only confuse the caller.

Connect with Empathy

Here's an experience that a friend of ours had; you may be able to relate to it:

My friend and I belong to a women's group that travels every year. We always make our reservations for a place to stay well in advance of the event.

When we checked into our hotel room, we noticed we had a king-size bed. Our call down to the front desk went something like this:

Me: We seem to have a mix-up with our rooms. We have a king-size bed instead of two doubles. We'd like to switch rooms.

Front Desk: We can't do that. The hotel is overbooked, so there are no rooms.

Me: Well, this isn't acceptable. I personally confirmed this and was assured we were all set.

Front Desk: Sorry, there's nothing we can do. We've overbooked.

Me: I made these reservations back in January. I called to confirm them last month, and again last week. This is not acceptable—you have to do something for us!

Front Desk: There's nothing we can do. The hotel is booked solid.

Me: Could you check a listing for Casey? She's with our party. Maybe we could switch rooms with her. It would make a big difference for us.

Front Desk:	We can't do that. She hasn't checked in yet.
Me:	Well, all the more reason to do it now.
Front Desk:	We can't do that. We have her name on the room.

What's going on here? What's the issue for our friend? True, she just wants the room she had confirmed. But it's more than that. Check out Front Desk's responses to that request. As the conversation proceeds, his words just add fuel to the fire.

What's missing in the front desk person's responses? Empathy. Empathy is the expression through words and tone that you understand the significance of an issue to someone else. You understand how he is affected by it and how he feels about it.

Empathy is not about feeling sorry. It's about recognizing how the other person is feeling. Imagine how things might have gone if the front desk clerk had said, "I can certainly understand your frustration, Ms. Gilbert, especially since you booked so long ago and confirmed the booking last week."

That's empathy. With that, the clerk shows that he "gets" what the customer is experiencing. Our friend may or may not have gotten the new room, but she would at least have felt that the hotel employee understood her.

THE IMPORTANCE OF EMPATHY

Why is empathy important? Because it is fundamental to making a connection. You want not only to respond to a caller's issue or problem but also to have the caller understand that you recognize the frustration, disappointment, even anger she feels in dealing with that issue or problem. That acknowledgment establishes a connection between you and the caller.

Just as important is an understanding of what empathy is not. It's not sympathy or pity. How many times have you heard these halfhearted attempts at empathy:

"I'm sorry you feel that way."

"I'm sorry you don't understand the process."

"I'm sorry to hear that."

These phrases don't express empathy. However well intentioned, they imply a distance between the speaker and the caller. In fact, you can even pick up on an implicit sense of blame in these comments. We often send unintended messages thinking that we're expressing empathy.

Here's the unintended message of those tragic phrases:

Unintended Messages

Rep says:	Subtle message received:
"I'm sorry you feel that way."	"It's your own fault you feel that way—you really shouldn't."
"I'm sorry you don't understand the process."	"It's perfectly clear to most people. I don't know why you don't get it."
"I'm sorry to hear that."	"Oh great—this means more work for me" or "Here we go again."

These kinds of messages are by no means what you're after.

Equally important, empathy is not agreement. When you express empathy, you do not need to agree with how the other person feels—rather, you acknowledge his feelings.

The expression of empathy helps establish relationships. Genuine empathy lets the caller know that you care enough to acknowledge how she is feeling. Moreover, you convey the message that you're genuinely there to help.

By demonstrating empathy, you recognize the other person as a human being. This makes him feel more comfortable with you and, therefore, more willing to work with you.

HOW TO EXPRESS EMPATHY

In a telephone conversation, you communicate empathy through two means: the tone of your voice and the words that you choose.

The most important tonal quality is one of sincerity. You are using your tone of voice to acknowledge the caller's feelings and to show a genuine desire to help her, so it is critical that you be sincere with your tone. The words you choose are of little help in establishing empathy if you sound bored or distracted or as if you are merely following a script.

When it comes to your choice of words, the first consideration is to use the appropriate level of empathy. For a "five-alarm fire" type of issue, give five-alarm empathy. For instance:

"Wow, it sounds like you have been through a lot lately. I can understand how you would be upset. I would be happy to help you."

If the issue is minor, give one-alarm empathy. For example:

"It sounds like this is important. I'd be glad to take care of this for you."

The goal is to use enough empathy to mirror your understanding of the person's feelings and the significance of the issue.

Too often representatives fall back on the "I'm sorry" or "I understand" catch phrases. Have you ever been on the receiving end of such "empathy"? The more frequently such phrases are uttered, the less empathic they feel. To develop your ability to convey sincere empathy, it is important for you to find the phrases that feel natural to you. Consider these:

"*I can understand* how that could be upsetting."

"*I recognize* that this is a difficult time for you."

"*I appreciate* your patience."

"*I realize* how important this is to you."

"*This sounds* urgent. I can help you right now."

There are many more examples, but you get the idea. The first step in expressing empathy to a caller is to point out that you acknowledge what he is feeling. Note the first few words of each empathy statement and find those that are comfortable for you.

From there, it is helpful to indicate how you intend to follow up on your expression of empathy. You can tell the caller that you plan to take action to help address her issue or concern. Or, if appropriate, you can ask for additional information that may prove useful. In either case, even the most upset or distraught customer is likely to feel better and to begin to communicate more effectively. From the caller's perspective, regardless of the outcome of the call, at least someone out there has a sense of what she is going through.

Take another quick look at the preceding examples of empathy. Note that every one of them expresses a sense of understanding. Not one expresses agreement.

Remember, empathy is about understanding the caller's point of view—not passing judgment on whether he is right or wrong.

There's another aspect of empathy that's important to remember. Looking back at our quick list of empathic expressions, you'll notice that all are focused on an issue or complaint that has the caller upset or frustrated. Empathy is important in those instances, but it's just as useful in more positive scenarios as well. Consider these phrases:

"Thanks for the compliment."

"I'm glad our product has worked so well for you."

"I'm happy that we were able to be of help today."

You needn't limit empathy just to problem solving or putting out fires. It's equally effective when a caller is on the line under happier circumstances. If that's the case, take advantage of empathy to share the caller's positive experience.

RESISTANCE TO EXPRESSING EMPATHY

There are two reasons why people tend to resist expressing empathy.

It Takes Too Long

We've heard people say, "I don't do empathy" or "Empathy takes too long" or "I want to get right to the job—that's what the customer wants."

There's no question that you need to address the task at hand; it is indeed an important matter. But the truth is that without empathy, your calls will actually take more time! The reason? If a customer doesn't sense that you "get it" and, instead, feels that you just seem to be focused on her account number or some other detail, she may think you didn't listen. That prompts her to continue to express emotion because she needs to know that you *do* get it. And all that takes time (not to mention further frustrates the caller).

Diffusing emotions by expressing empathy at the beginning of a conversation calms customers down. Then they're more willing to work with you, which makes the process smoother and less time-consuming. Try it—it will reduce the length of your calls, not to mention your stress level.

What If I Don't Get It Right?

This is a legitimate concern. But think of it in this way: a genuine attempt to understand a caller's emotion, delivered in the right tone, is almost always appreciated for what it is—genuine. It's possible that you identify a customer's feeling as "upset," and the caller corrects you by telling you he's frustrated. So be it. He will perceive your words as a sincere attempt to acknowledge what he's experiencing.

A **MAGIC** Moment

Empathy can flow in two directions. Even when you are the customer, you can make a difference by empathizing with your service provider. The following story from one of our associates shows that expressing empathy can pay off in more ways than one.

"Maryann stopped at a local office-supply store to get an article laminated. There were only a few customers in the store, one of whom happened to be in front of her in line. This customer was mailing a few packages and refused to cooperate with the store associate. The customer was barking curt responses to the associate's questions and sighing heavily as the associate attempted to complete the task with little assistance.

"Anxious to get to work on time, Maryann quickly realized that she was behind the 'wrong' person. Her first impulse was to share some less than complimentary comments with the resistant customer. Instead, she paused briefly and recognized that any comment to this person would not help the situation. Then she smiled at the store associate and showed, through her expression, that she understood what he was going through. When he had finished with the curt customer, she said, 'Wow, that was a tough situation for you.' He nodded and then apologized for the delay and immediately laminated her article. As he handed her the finished product, he announced that it was free of charge—just because she was patient and understanding."

As customers, people too often lose sight of the impression they make and the impact of their resistance on the situation. A little empathy can go a long way—whether someone is the rep *or* the customer.

MAGIC **Maxims**

- Empathy involves recognizing and acknowledging what a person is feeling and expressing.
- Empathy is not agreement.
- You can establish or restore a relationship with empathy.
- Using empathy will help shorten service interactions.

chapter SEVEN

Build Customer Confidence

N ow's the time to establish credibility so that the person at the other end of the line begins to have faith in you and your willingness and ability to help. In a sense, you're ensuring that the person will want to talk with you again in the future.

THE NAME IS THE GAME

Because so many people and companies emphasize account numbers and the like as the first means of identification, take a few minutes to picture the following:

You are sitting in a café waiting to meet a business associate for the first time. The newcomer walks up to you, smiles, extends his hand, looks you directly in the eye, and says, "You must be 24657-6541; it's a pleasure to meet you!"

What happens? It's possible you may burst into laughter, and justifiably so. Calling someone by a number in that fashion is absurd. It's tough to keep a straight face.

But chances are also good that you'll experience something a good deal less pleasant: you may feel depersonalized, even dehumanized. You're not a name; you're 24657-6541.

This scenario may sound strange, but it's just what occurs in many settings when callers are asked for a number before they are addressed as a person. No matter if the rep is asking for an account number, a Social Security number, or any other such means of numeric identification, it's a cold approach that puts the caller off. And, from the standpoint of serving that caller, it's also grossly ineffective. She wants two things: (1) a professional who sincerely wants to help her and (2) to have her problem solved.

The rep just wants a number.

Happily there's a simple way to skirt the problems that an emphasis on numbers and other forms of impersonal behavior can create: use the name of the person on the other end of the line just as soon as you hear it.

To put it simply, a person's name is the very antithesis of a number. It is his and his alone. In fact, it's everyone's favorite word! And by using it the first chance you get, you're recognizing that person as important—and deserving of your attention.

Because you've brought things to a more personal level by using the person's name, chances are good she's going to listen more attentively to the conversation and provide more substantial input. That can certainly save you time and make your job a whole lot easier and more enjoyable.

A **MAGIC** Moment

Never underestimate the importance of using another person's name at your first opportunity. Consider this story from a colleague of ours trained in MAGIC:

"On a recent flight, I was startled by the sound of the captain over the intercom. He sounded stressed as he announced, 'Anyone with medical training, please come to the front of the plane immediately for a sick passenger.'

"Having been an emergency medical technician for twenty-two years, I thought I should go forward quickly. I expected there would be several other volunteers, but it turned out that I was the only one.

"The passenger looked very pale and only semiconscious. Noticing the panicked look on the faces surrounding me, I took a deep breath.

" 'My name is George, and I am here to help you,' I said to her, making sure it was loud enough so others could also hear. 'May I ask your name, please?'

"She said her name was Barbara, and I continued. 'Barbara, I can help you right away. First, I need to ask you a few questions. Is that OK?' She replied a weak yes.

"I quickly learned that she was a diabetic who had not eaten or taken her meds all day. I was able to help her so that she felt much better. The situation in hand, we didn't have to divert the flight to a closer airport. In fact, at the end of the flight as I was walking off with her, the captain thanked me for my professionalism and quick action.

"But I knew it was more than that. By giving Barbara my name and quickly getting hers in return, I had made the necessary connection with her so I could move quickly to find out what I needed to know. Even better, by proceeding as I did, I could feel the tension of the crowd around me subside as they gained confidence that I did know what I was doing."

Granted, not every instance of hearing and using another person's name is a matter of life and death. But no matter the setting, the exchange of names is essential in establishing a bond of confidence and trust.

THE ART OF NAME CAPTURE

Sometimes, finding out the name of the person at the other end of the phone line is rather simple. He gives it to you. However straightforward that might be, it places the onus on you to be ready. Listen carefully to see if the caller does offer his name. If he does, write it down. If it's unusual, ask him to spell it and, if need be, request a phonetic pronunciation.

For a variety of reasons, some callers don't volunteer their names. Maybe they prefer a degree of anonymity, or they're so focused on sharing their issue that they simply forget to say who they are.

If that happens, it's up to you to ask. Watch for your first opportunity, then politely ask for the caller's name. Typically this should be the first question you ask. Once you hear the name, use it immediately. This builds that personal connection between you and the caller. Be mindful of your tone when you ask for the name. You do not want the request to sound like an attack or interrogation. If your company has a policy of asking for the name, be aware that because you ask for names day in and day out, your tone could sound rote and mechanical.

Just how should you address the caller? Listen to her with care, as she will often tell you. If the caller happens to offer a title or some other specific form of address, take care to use it exactly as it's given to you. The following are some examples:

Doctor Nanji

Rabbi Goldstein

Mr. Nelson

Mrs. Kaplan

Ms. Rogers

A caller who recognizes that you took the time to pick up on how he prefers to be addressed is someone who's going to feel confident that his needs will be addressed. That furthers the connection and confidence that you've already begun to build.

Here are a couple more tips that can prove helpful with regard to using a caller's name. If, by chance, a caller offers his first and last name without your asking, you can solidify the personal nature of the call by using his first name from there on. If that's not something with which you feel entirely comfortable, you can say, "May I call you Jim?" or some other polite means of asking for permission.

If, however, you have to ask for the caller's name, it's best to stay with a more formal approach, such as "Mrs. Mercer" or "Mr. McAuliffe." The reasoning is simple: someone who didn't volunteer her name possibly wants to keep the conversation at arm's length, at least initially. With that in mind, you are better off keeping things on your end equally formal until you've established a more substantive sense of confidence.

One final note: we generally recommend using names instead of "Sir" and "Ma'am." A lot of people prefer not to be addressed in this manner, and such forms of address can also lend an impersonal feeling to a conversation. Far better to use a person's name in most cases.

A **MAGIC** Moment

Sometimes you may learn a customer's name in an indirect way, but it's still just as important. Here's a MAGIC anecdote from a friend of ours:

"I've belonged to a lot of fitness clubs in my life. The last two were small, women-only clubs. Much to my dismay, both of these clubs closed their doors suddenly. I couldn't bear the thought of this happening again, so I joined one of those 'mega clubs' with multiple locations.

"I expected a colder, less personal experience, yet I found the complete opposite to be true. When you enter this club, the front desk associate always greets you with a smile. But it gets better. A couple of the front desk associates have noted my name and have used it every time I enter or leave the club.

"I have even seen these same associates at different clubs that are part of this mega club (I go to three different locations), and they still call me by name. In fact, they make an effort to greet me and offer to help. One time, I was running late to class, and another front desk associate was about to ask for my name so that she could check me into the system. My 'friend' at the club stopped her and said, 'That is Cathy, and I will check her in. Please go on in and enjoy your class, Cathy.'

"The funny thing is, she has met hundreds of people at this club and yet she remembers my name.

"I feel special when I go there. In fact, it's a much more comfortable and personal experience than I ever had at those smaller clubs."

Even though this anecdote is about a face-to-face situation, the same rules apply when you are dealing with someone on the phone. The story reinforces the power of calling others by their name and illustrates that if you're attentive, opportunities to obtain a name don't always have to boil down to simply asking.

OFFERING HELP

If you think back to the story of the airline passenger who assisted a sick woman, you can see that his offering his name and obtaining hers in return were essential to moving the interaction forward to where it ultimately needed to go— and fast.

That goal was *help*. The gentleman with EMT training wasted no time in letting the woman know that he was there to help her.

When dealing with others on the phone, you can do the exact same thing. Let your caller know that you're there to help in any way you can. On the surface, going to the seeming trouble of informing your caller that you will help her may appear a bit silly or, at the very least, unnecessary. After all, that's what you're there for, right?

The problem is that a readiness to help—and letting the other person know of that readiness in no uncertain terms—often gets buried in many conversations. Instead of saying they'll help, people ask for account numbers. For passwords. For serial numbers. Granted, those requests may be part of the resolution process, but they certainly don't come across as helpful if they are the first thing a customer hears—particularly if he is unhappy or upset.

A **MAGIC** Moment

Here's an actual call from one of our training files that beautifully illustrates the paramount importance of saying you intend to help the caller:

Phone Rep: Good afternoon, this is Jake. May I help you?

Caller (*clearly peeved*): I want to speak to your supervisor!

Rep: My name is Jake, and I can help you right now. May I ask you . . .

Caller: No, you may not ask me! I am sick and tired of getting the runaround from you people. Getting different answers to the same question every time I call!

Rep: I know how annoying that can be and can see that we have created a very frustrating situation for you. I want to help you with this and get you the information you need. My name is Jake, and I am here to help you right now. May I ask who I am speaking with, please?

Caller: I'm Elmer Gomez, and I'm looking for a competent person to help me straighten this out.

Rep: Mr. Gomez, I assure you that I can help. I will do everything I can to straighten this out. Would it be all right if I ask a few questions so I can understand what you need?

There are a few important points to note here. First, the rep's immediate presentation of his name to begin establishing a connection with the caller. Then—just as important—his repeated assertion that he wanted to help the caller immediately. And it worked! With his decision to give his name, the caller demonstrated his growing confidence that the rep was competent and, in fact, ready to help him in any way he possibly could.

Equally important to note in that MAGIC Moment were those things that the rep did *not* say. There was no mention of account numbers or anything that moved the conversation away from establishing a personal connection. Rather than addressing the actual problem itself, the rep focused on putting the relationship first by connecting with the caller's experience of the situation—in other words, through empathy. This strategy not only soothed the caller's emotions but also reassured him that the rep could help.

As we've illustrated, a caller who isn't comfortable with a rep's intentions or abilities may feel frustrated. The word *frustration* literally means "to cause to bring to no effect." If a person is frustrated, whatever she is doing isn't likely to go particularly well. This is especially true when she is communicating with someone. One of the first things to go out the door is her ability to listen to or really hear what the other person is saying. If you do not attend to or acknowledge the frustration of the caller, you increase your chances of making mistakes, lengthening the call, and having to deal with callbacks that could have been avoided.

MAGIC WORDS—HOW TO SAY YOU'LL HELP

Here are a few examples of MAGIC phrases that convey, without any undue scripting, a concrete willingness to help:

"I can help you with that right now."

"I can look into that for you."

"I will take care of that for you."

"I'd be glad to help you."

"I'd be happy to research that."

Although obviously different from each other, all these phrases let the other person know, "You and I are on the same side of the table. You may be a number in a lot of other places, but here I took the time to obtain your name and to establish your faith in my commitment to help."

Please also note that these phrases go beyond establishing a clear commitment to help: they are uniformly positive in tone and delivery. The specific words that make up each phrase—*happy, certain, glad,* and others like them—reinforce the message itself by building a positive, constructive environment, one that focuses on helping resolve the issue at hand.

"HELP" DEFINED

One of the problems that some people may have with saying that they can help is fear of misrepresentation. Put another way, they don't want to claim they can help someone when in fact they believe that they won't be able to.

That's natural; not every person has every solution, and to suggest otherwise would indeed be misleading. But help in this instance isn't a literal guarantee of a solution. Have another look at the MAGIC phrases we just cited—never in any one of them does the rep say anything that even hints that the problem is as good as solved.

Rather, all that the reps do say is that they're willing and ready to help. Telling someone at the other end of the telephone line that you intend to help him means just that: you are going to help, and you are committed to working toward resolution. You may not be able to resolve the issue directly, such as by sending the caller a check or answering a complicated legal question, but you can always move things a step forward—connecting him with the right person or conducting additional research. To put it another way: you may not get him from A to Z—representing the ultimate solution—but you can always get him to B (the next step). With that in mind, you can always say "I can help you" with the utmost confidence.

Such a statement not only is straightforward and encouraging to the caller but also establishes the phone representative as a genuine professional—one who cares about what she does and is willing to do everything she can to further that commitment. Think back to when you heard a phone rep ask for your account number at the outset of a call. Did it sound professional or merely like a blasé, rote response? By contrast, think of the impression you get when a rep says that she'll help you.

A **MAGIC** Moment

Never overlook the importance of offering to help—even if, of necessity, the offer to help appears somewhat later rather than earlier. A friend told this story:

"Dealing with a certain wireless carrier was an incredibly frustrating experience for several months. After noticing a mistake on my bill, I called customer service to notify them about the error. My first contact was with a seemingly bored rep who said she would take care of the error. When I got my next statement and found that the error had not been fixed and that I was charged a late fee since I had not paid the amount in question, I was very annoyed.

"I called back and got another indifferent rep who, after hearing my emotional plea, just asked for my account number. After waiting for what seemed like an eternity, he came back to tell me that the late fee was justified and that there were no notes about my previous call. Therefore I was 'wrong,' and the mistake on the bill was not a mistake at all.

"This went on for another three months—until I got Martha on the line. I ranted and raved at Martha for a few minutes, telling her of the ridiculous mistake and the fact that they keep charging me late fees on an amount that was their error in the first place. Martha listened and then said, 'It sounds like you've had quite a frustrating experience with us. I'd be happy to look into this for you.'

"'Finally—someone who's caring and capable!' I said to myself. The impact of Martha's words was immediate. I felt relieved, listened to, calmer, and more confident that the error would be fixed—just because of those nine words."

THE NEXT STEP: ASKING PERMISSION TO GET MORE INFORMATION

Gaining additional information is essential to dealing with an issue or solving a problem, but there's a world of difference among the ways you can get that information. If you just go ahead and start asking questions, the other person may not know where you are going. She may think you're intruding or poking your nose into areas in which she thinks you have no business. She can also feel as though she were being interrogated or led in a direction that may not solve her problem.

You can avoid all this by asking permission first. For one thing, the caller is likely to feel more at ease and less intimidated. Moreover, you are being courteous; you're asking the caller if it's OK to find out more than what you have so far. But, just as important, asking for permission lets you assume the lead of the conversation. By granting her OK for you to ask questions, the caller has put you in charge of the direction of the conversation in a very natural and comfortable fashion. You are now ready to gain the information you need.

Here are a few examples of specific ways to ask permission:

"To ensure accuracy, I'd like to ask for some clarifying information. Would that be OK?"

"I'm sure I can help you with that. May I ask you a few questions first?"

"The quickest way I can help you is to get a little more information. Would that be all right?"

You get the idea. By now, you've established a comfortable environment in which to proceed to addressing the caller's needs.

By the way, if you need to ask only one question, there's really no need to ask permission to do so—that's a bit of overkill. Imagine hearing this: "May I ask one question so that I can correct your account information? May I have your new address?" That's unnecessary.

There's always the possibility that a caller will say no—often in rather blunt terms—when you ask for more information. That's perfectly OK—it's clear that he hasn't vented enough or felt listened to or understood. The best strategy: just listen, respond with as much empathy as appropriate, keep using his name, and let him know you're there to help. Chances are good that he'll come around when he is convinced you are a professional who is there to help him. At that point, ask permission to gain more information, and you are on your way, in the driver's seat with a willing passenger.

MAGIC **Maxims**

- Use the customer's name as soon as you hear it.
- At the start of the interaction, tell the caller that you will help.
- Ask permission to gain more information when you need to ask several questions.

MAGIC Words and Phrases

To this point, we have addressed the M in MAGIC: "Make a Connection." Now it's time to move on to the next of the five MAGIC steps: "Act Professionally: Express Confidence."

Many customers are dissatisfied with the service they receive, describing it as indifferent or routine. By acting professionally, you can directly influence customers' perception of your service—and, in so doing, create a more positive experience. Your words, tone, pace, clarity, and volume all contribute to this experience. In this chapter, we focus on the words themselves.

WHAT MAKES A WORD OR PHRASE MAGIC?

MAGIC words and phrases contribute to strengthening the connection with the customer. They convey sincere attention and respect.

So, what makes words and phrases MAGIC? One of three things:

1. **They're personal.** To make a connection with a caller—and, from there, to establish both confidence and empathy—you need to personalize the call. These personalizing words and phrases can be as simple as the customer's name or congratulations for a recent happy event.

2. **They're specific.** Stay away from statements like this: "Hey, Jim, I know you're waiting on that information, so I'll try to get it to you, whenever, I'm not sure when . . ." These words are vague and confusing, and they can be rather unsettling to an upset customer. We suggest you be specific and provide time frames and details that matter to the customer.

3. **They're empathic.** You should be familiar with this one: "Jim, that sounds as though it was really a frustrating experience." As we pointed out in Chapter Six, empathy is essential to establishing connection as well as confidence and trust.

Let's look now at some words and phrases that are personal, specific, and empathic.

BE PERSONAL

By using words and phrases like those here, you make a personal connection with your customers. This makes them feel significant, that they are not just a number to a large institution.

"Congratulations on your promotion!"

"I'm very glad I was able to help you with this, Ms. Silverman."

"My name is Mary Kaplan. Please do feel free to call me again if you need any further assistance."

Let's take a look at the difference personal phrases can make. We'll start with a conversation *without* personal MAGIC phrases:

Customer:	This is Mrs. Sankar, and I'm calling because there's a late charge, and I know I sent my payment in on time.
Rep:	OK, what's your account number?
Customer:	1234567.
Rep:	OK, what's the mistake?
Customer:	There's a late charge, and I know I sent my payment in on time.
Rep:	We'll take a look and get back to you.

Now consider the same interchange *with* personal MAGIC phrases:

Customer:	This is Mrs. Sankar, and I'm calling because there's a late charge, and I know I sent my payment in on time.
Rep:	Mrs. Sankar, I'd be happy to look into that for you. May I ask a few questions so I may help you more quickly?

Customer:	Certainly.
Rep:	May I have your account number please?
Customer:	Yes, it's 1234567.
Rep:	That's 1234567. I do see the late charge and would be glad to look into that for you.

You can see that being personal helps you connect with the customer.

Referring to the prior example, you'll see that the rep used the customer's name. That's an important part of being personal. As we've noted, people love to hear the sound of their own name. They feel like a human being with needs and concerns—not a number.

You can also make this kind of connection by using courtesies and affirmative statements (for example, "please" and "thank you"). These demonstrate respect and create a positive tone for the conversation.

A note about please and thank you: these so-called common courtesies are not always that common. We all learned them as young children, yet somehow they seem to disappear from many of our conversations. Why do we expect so much from our children but don't expect the same of ourselves? Start listening for the use of these small courtesies in the conversations around you. Notice the difference they make.

BE SPECIFIC

Being specific is a way to "take ownership" of the conversation. Use your name and say what you will do to help. This helps put the caller at ease and lets him know that he is working with a professional.

Specifically identifying *how* you will help and *when* creates a sense of trust and confidence between you and the caller. When she first called, she might not have been sure just what might happen—if indeed anything at all. Now, thanks to MAGIC words and phrases that emphasize specificity, she knows who is going to help her, when, and exactly how that's going to happen.

"I will fax the form to you in five minutes."

"I will contact the Underwriting Department today to get more information on your claim, and I will call you with an update by 5:00 PM Pacific time tomorrow."

"I can take care of your address change right now. Your August statement will be sent to your 143 Red Rose Lane address."

BE EMPATHIC

As we discussed in Chapter Six, MAGIC phrases can be empathic. Here are a few more examples of empathic phrases that demonstrate professionalism:

"You have been very patient. Thank you."

"You sound upset. Please tell me exactly what happened."

"You have a right to be concerned. I will look into this matter right now."

And we want to remind you again that empathy also works in positive situations:

"I'm so glad the software is working so well for you."

"That sounds like a terrific way to use our product!"

In any situation, empathy means you understand and appreciate a caller's issues or circumstances.

Experiment with MAGIC

Think about your own interactions with customers. What opportunities do you have to use MAGIC phrases? Remember—even the most mundane conversation can be enhanced with these phrases.

A MAGIC Moment

A friend shared the following story about a rep who gave great service and delivered as promised:

"I was having a problem with my DSL modem, so I called the provider to get it fixed. He led me through a troubleshooting process. He was very understanding throughout the entire call. First, he empathized by saying how frustrating it was when your Internet server was down—we even laughed about how much we depended on it these days!

"He eventually determined that the problem was a bad router and that he needed to set up a service visit. It was scheduled for the following week. (He even set a deadline without my having to ask.) When I said I would rather have the modem sent to me so I would fix it more quickly, he responded, 'I can certainly do that for you, Sondra. If you don't mind, I will take down some information so I can overnight it to you.'

"The modem arrived the next day. I will definitely stick with this provider. These days, it's very hard to find one that delivers the goods and gives great service, too."

MAGIC **Maxims**

- Using MAGIC phrases will improve your customers' perception of you and your organization.
- MAGIC phrases are
  - Personal—they emphasize use of names and accountability.
  - Specific—they tell the customer what you're going to do and when.
  - Empathic—they let the customer know that you understand what her experience is like.
- MAGIC phrases connect you with your customer and show that you genuinely care and want to help.

chapter NINE

Tragic Words and Phrases

W̲e all recognize that the words we use can affect how others see us. But every day, many of us use phrases that can chip away at our credibility—and at a customer's service experience.

We call these tragic phrases. They are phrases that

- Put distance between the representative and the customer
- Create uneasiness
- Imply a lack of action or responsibility
- Are impersonal
- Are vague or unclear
- Use inappropriate slang

A **Tragic** Moment

Have a look at a tragic experience that a friend of ours had to go through.

"I needed an audio cassette recorder, so I went to a well-known electronics establishment. A store associate helped me select one he thought would meet my needs. This device came packaged in a molded plastic casing that must be cut apart to remove the device for actual use.

"The performance of this device was nothing short of terrible. I elected to exchange it for a different model.

"When I approached the counter with the new recorder, I had to wave an associate over from the other side of the counter, as he appeared to be ignoring me. He then motioned to the manager, who came to 'help' me. The manager's name tag had 'Elite Status' printed on it.

"He asked me a number of questions about how I was using the recorder. As I answered his questions, he began to replace the batteries and proceeded to test the machine. (I was beginning to feel like he thought I didn't know how to use a tape recorder.) Eventually I reiterated that the device wasn't broken and that I just wanted to exchange it for this different model.

"The manager replied that for him to do anything for me, he would need the original packaging. I let him know that I did not have that because I had to cut it open and that that packaging would now be useless to him anyway.

"He then held up my receipt displaying the back side full of fine print—literally, right in my face. He said, 'If you had read our return policy, you would know that all returns require their original packaging or they are not accepted.' In disbelief, I said, 'I had to destroy the case just to get the device out. That package is useless!'

"He then reluctantly said he'd be willing to discuss it further if I could at least produce the owner's manual. But until that happened, he wouldn't help me.

"At that point, I gave up and went across the street to the competition.

"I'll never buy from that particular location of this electronics store again. Apparently, Mr. Elite Status let his name tag go to his head."

Where's the "tragic" in this anecdote? Let us count the ways:

- Confrontational words: "If you had read our return policy . . ."
- Condescending questions that suggested our friend couldn't operate a simple tape recorder.
- Outright refusal to help.

There are additional examples—both in speech as well as in action—but this incident of tragic behavior is about as subtle as getting beaned with a two-by-four. From the very outset of the conversation, the manager appears to be steadfast in his overall posture of refusal—a refusal to listen to our friend and appreciate his perspective, let alone provide any alternatives.

Also notice:

- There's no attempt at any type of personal contact or interaction; there is instead an ongoing deferral to abstract "policy" that's made to sound like one of the Ten Commandments.

- There's no specificity, no sense that the manager cares about addressing the situation at hand. Instead of asking specific questions geared to identifying why this particular machine didn't fit the customer's needs, the manager gave the impression that our friend was some sort of nitwit who—provided he had even a sliver of intelligence—could easily make this tape recorder work properly.

- Certainly, there isn't a hint of empathy to be found anywhere—no attempt whatsoever on the manager's part to find common ground from which to build a fair and equitable solution.

The bottom line of this series of tragic missteps? Our friend's concern was never addressed. The most tragic result of all: our friend will never step inside that store again and will likely tell others of this unpleasant experience (after all, he told us!).

Tragic indeed.

To take your understanding of tragic words and expressions further, here's a sampling of actual tragic phrases we have heard in customer interactions. We've categorized them as sloppy, noncommittal, or authoritarian. See how many are familiar to you.

Sloppy

"Hold on" or "Hang on."

"What's your problem?"

"Just a sec."

"Here's what I'm gonna do . . ."

". . . pull you up" (on my screen).

Noncommittal

"I can't do that" or "We can't do that."

"He's very busy now."

"That's not my department. You'll have to speak with someone else."

"I don't know."

"We'll have to call you back."

Authoritarian

"You have to . . ." or "You should have . . ."

"That's against company policy."

"Calm down."

"Like I said . . ."

"If you had read your manual . . ."

There are a variety of unfortunate themes and characteristics that weave their mischief through these phrases. First off, they're all impersonal; instead of bringing the rep closer to the customer, these suggest a sense of distance, a lack of connection.

They also share a sense of rigidity—a "my way or the highway" intransigence. It's a communications form of brinkmanship. Either you can like it, or you can lump it. End of story.

SUBTLE TRAGIC WORDS AND PHRASES

Unlike our earlier tragic example, which was about as low-key as a nuclear blast, these are a bit more subtle. What makes the following phrases tragic? The speakers' implied messages, shown in the right column, are good clues.

Tragic Phrase	Implied Message
"As soon as possible."	"When I get around to it."
"I'll try."	"Not sure I can do it."
"The truth is . . ."	"I probably shouldn't tell you this."
"To be honest . . ."	"I was lying up until now."
"Hopefully . . ."	"Who really knows?"
"Maybe" or "Possibly."	"I really have no idea."

Another form of a subtle yet commonly used tragic phrase is the use of the word "we." How many times have you heard a rep say,

"We'll call you back."

"We'll take care of that for you."

"We'll ship the product in one to two weeks."

"We need your account number to do that."

Using "we" can sound vague; it can leave the customer wondering who will take action and who to call for follow-up. It can also sound as though you, the rep, have little or nothing to do with the next steps, nor do you care very much about the matter.

If you are indeed the one who is responsible for an action, then use "I" to convey that personal accountability. Instead of the tragic statements just listed, you could say,

"I will call tomorrow at 4:00 PM."

"I will personally take care of that for you."

"The product takes one to two weeks to ship. I will put the request in today."

"May I please have your account number so that I can investigate this further?"

"We" can be used to indicate a team, organization, or company. If you wish to use it in this context, it is important to identify specifically to whom the "we" is referring. For example:

"The development team will be exploring your issue."

"The underwriting department will need approximately a week to investigate."

OTHER FORMS OF TRAGIC LANGUAGE

Obvious and subtle aren't the only means by which tragic language can surface. Consider a couple of additional suspects:

Slang. It is always a good practice to avoid slang in conversations—even in informal settings. Saying "yeah," "gotcha," "you betcha," "awesome," and other like expressions can bring your professionalism into question.

Jargon and acronyms. Any industry-specific terminology or acronym that a customer cannot understand is jargon. When you spend a good deal of time in a particular setting or environment, it's easy to begin using insider terminology. That can include everything from highly technical terminology to abbreviations and colloquial expressions.

This may be fine for the folks on the inside, but may not work with customers and others with little or no exposure to those expressions. To them, your jargon may be completely incomprehensible. And that can lead to a tragic breakdown in communication.

If you're certain a customer understands a term, go ahead and use it. One way to determine this is to listen carefully to a customer's responses in a conversation. You may notice that he understands your terminology and in fact may use it himself.

Rule of thumb: if 95 percent of the general public understands a word or phrase, it's OK to use. When in doubt, just use simpler language to explain a term's meaning.

A **Tragic** Moment

This story from one of our facilitators highlights how a cashier's choice of language affected the facilitator's experience and future buying decisions.

"When I was a loan officer, I would seek out referrals from people I knew in different businesses. I liked to bring them little gifts, like candy, to show my appreciation. When I saw that a national department store chain near me had a 90 percent off sale on their Halloween items, I knew it was a great time to shop for those gifts.

"I went to this store and was thrilled with the selection, and started picking up all sorts of items. Soon my hands were full, so I put some stuff down at a register and went back to get more of these great inexpensive gifts.

"One cashier looked at me and then exclaimed for all to hear, 'Take that ghost out of your purse!' I couldn't believe it—she was accusing me of shoplifting! I told her that she could look in my purse and see for herself that there was no ghost in there. She refused.

"I was so embarrassed—everyone was looking at me, though I knew I had done nothing wrong. I paid for my items with cash so that I could get out of that store as quickly as possible.

"When I got home, I realized that the cashier's accusation may have been illegal, and it was certainly not the right thing to do. I decided that somebody at the store needed to know how I was treated. I called the manager and told her that I was humiliated and upset by the experience. The manager's response surprised me. She didn't listen at all. She kept cutting me off, saying, 'I wish you had talked to me before you left the store' and 'I'm going to talk to that cashier about this.' She didn't even ask for my name, and she certainly didn't apologize for the incident. It seemed that she couldn't care less about me. All she had to do was apologize and say something like, 'I can see how that would have been humiliating,' and I would have felt much better. But she didn't—and I felt worse!

"I never went back to that store, and I tell every participant in every MAGIC program about that experience and the lost opportunity to save a customer."

HOW TO AVOID TRAGIC WORDS AND EXPRESSIONS

Having gone through a variety of tragic words and phrases, you may justifiably be asking, "OK, what can I do about them?"

First, pinpoint the tragic words and phrases you tend to use. Then choose alternative language and practice it in your conversations. For instance:

Instead of: "You've got the wrong number."

Use: "I'm sorry, you've reached the billing department. I would be happy to connect you to . . ."

Instead of: "She not here right now."

Use: "She's in a meeting now, and I expect her back by three. I'll see that she receives your message then. Or, if you prefer, I would be happy to put you through to her voicemail."

These examples show how being personal, being specific, and showing empathy (as we discussed in Chapter Eight) can transform any phrase, however tragic, into one that establishes a genuine connection between you and the customer.

Experiment with MAGIC

Following are some commonly used tragic phrases (some rather subtle). Consider how these phrases might apply in your service environment. Then decide how you would reword them to make them MAGIC. Our suggested MAGIC makeovers follow this section.

Tragic Phrase	Your MAGIC Alternative
"I'll call as soon as possible."	
"I'd like to help, but . . ."	
"Unfortunately, those aren't in stock."	
"I'll have to check with my supervisor."	
"Why don't you call back later?"	
"Our system can't do that."	
"I'll see what I can do."	
"I'll try to find the file."	
"Hopefully, it'll arrive."	
"You have to understand . . ."	
"Who's calling?"	
"To be honest with you . . ."	
"Possibly."	
"Obviously, you missed the deadline."	

On a final note, think of some tragic phrases, tech speak, or jargon you use every day. Jot them down and see how you can make them MAGIC. Remember, the key to moving your conversations from tragic to MAGIC is awareness and practice.

MAGIC **Makeovers**

Take a look at the following examples of tragic phrases transformed into MAGIC phrases:

Tragic Phrase	MAGIC Phrase
"I'll call as soon as possible."	"I will call by 3 PM."
"I'd like to help, but . . ."	"What I can do is . . ."
"Unfortunately, those aren't in stock."	"Those are not in stock right now, but I will find out when the next shipment is due."
"I'll have to check with my supervisor."	"I'd be happy to check that. Would you mind holding while I do that?"
"Why don't you call back later?"	"Do you mind calling back after you've spoken with your attorney?"
"Our system can't do that."	"Our system is not able to receive live video transmissions."
"I'll see what I can do."	"What I'm going to do is . . ."
"I'll try to find the file."	"It will take a little while to gather this information. May I call you back in an hour with more details?"
"Hopefully, it'll arrive."	"It is scheduled to arrive at 4:00 PM."
"You have to understand . . ."	"I'd like to explain this another way to make it more clear."
"Who's calling?"	"May I ask who's calling?"
"To be honest with you . . ."	"To be candid with you . . ."
"Possibly."	"I will do my utmost to see that this gets to you."
"Obviously, you missed the deadline."	"Since it's past the deadline, the best thing to do is . . ."

MAGIC **Maxims**

- A tragic word or phrase is negative in some fashion. It creates distance between you and your customer.

- Tragic words and expressions show little or no empathy or specificity and are impersonal in nature.

- Jargon and acronyms can also be tragic.

- Careful rephrasing can make a tragic word or phrase into a MAGIC one.

- Catching yourself and rephrasing tragic wording to MAGIC wording will uplift your conversations and help you make a more positive impression.

PART FOUR

Express MAGIC Accountability

Voicemail

U p to this point in the book, we have examined interactions that are "live" conversations, ones that go back and forth between you and someone else. Let's now take a quick break to address another form of communication, which can prove no less essential to customer relationships.

We're talking about voicemail—both the message you have on your phone to field calls from others and the messages you leave on other people's machines and systems.

Like other means of communicating with others, voicemail genuinely matters when it comes to building and sustaining positive relationships with customers.

A professional voicemail positions you as responsive and genuinely interested in helping the caller. It also can save valuable time that would otherwise be lost through phone tag and calls returned with insufficient guidance or information.

Clear, courteous, and concise voicemail messages can work wonders. Inadequate messages can wreak havoc, as you'll see in the following example.

A **Tragic** Moment

A client (who worked at a large financial services organization) shared a true story of how a standard voicemail greeting cost the company a lot of money.

"One of the company's personal bankers had a very standard voicemail message. The message didn't say how long he would be out of the office or if someone else was available to help. It sounded like this: 'Hi, this is John Smith.

I'm not here right now. Leave me a message and I'll get back to you as soon as possible.' This turned out to be a 'tragic' mistake.

"One of his high-worth clients called in the morning and left a message for a callback—he assumed the banker had just stepped away from his desk. When he didn't hear back, he called again that afternoon and left a second message.

"The banker came in the next morning and returned the call in the afternoon. The client said, 'You can meet me at the bank in twenty minutes. I'm coming to take out all my money. Clearly, I need you more than you need me.' He then came and took out all seven million dollars in his account!"

Had the voicemail message been more specific, the client may have reacted differently. Instead, the bank lost one of its biggest customers.

Experiment with MAGIC

To get a handle on what constitutes an effective voicemail message, you'll benefit from seeing where you are now.

When you record your outgoing greeting on the voicemail system, you no doubt give it a quick listen to make sure you haven't left out anything or provided inaccurate information. Now you're going to take that everyday task a step further by listening—really listening—to the type of outgoing message you leave for others via your voicemail system.

To do that, call your own number and listen carefully to your voicemail message as if you were a customer calling for the first time.

What is your general reaction? How does the message make you feel? (Recall the signal-light analogy we discussed in Chapter Five.) How does it influence what you feel about the person or the company that's represented? Further, will it affect the response you might leave?

YOU'RE NOT THERE, BUT YOU ARE

One simple aspect of voicemail can lead to unintended problems: when the call comes in, you're somewhere else.

That makes your voicemail your temporary representative, your surrogate. And, as such, your voicemail must represent you in the very best light; you want it to provide the best service possible, just as you would wish to do were you there in the flesh.

Keep in mind that voicemail communication is one-way. When greeting a customer on the phone, you can sometimes give the wrong impression at first, but fortunately you can overcome that impression later in the same conversation.

Voicemail also makes an impression, but if the impression is not positive, you don't have the ability to change it until a later time, when you can interact directly with the customer. By the same token, when you leave a voicemail message, you can't change it. You have just that one chance to manage the impression.

Having an effective outgoing voicemail message will establish a climate that sets up further contact with callers. You want to make sure that they want to contact you again—even if their initial exposure to you consisted of just a few seconds of a recorded greeting.

CREATE A PERSONAL, EFFECTIVE OUTGOING VOICEMAIL

The goal of any effective voicemail is to provide the caller with sufficient information so that she is in a position to make the best possible decision she can—be that simply leaving a message, contacting someone else, or choosing some other option.

You want to be as specific and as thorough as you can, providing personal and helpful information that the caller can put to immediate use.

Here's a breakdown of some of the components that make up an effective and personal outgoing voicemail:

1. **Offer a salutation.** Use your first and last names for complete clarity (or just your first name if that's what your organization prefers). You can also let the caller know the location he has reached.

2. **Provide the date.** Ever leave someone a voicemail, only to find out that she was out on vacation for a month—and that her message had overlooked that bit of information? (Or, even worse, the message says she's off for the week for Christmas break, and you just bought some Fourth of July sparklers?)

Don't make that mistake with yours. When recording your message, give the date. Just as important, update your message regularly.

3. **Let callers know why you're not there.** To exceed customer expectations, it's only appropriate that you let callers know why you're not around to take their call personally. It may be a day that you're in the office but are merely temporarily unavailable. But instead you may be in Madagascar for the next six months. So let callers know why you're not there to pick up the phone. Use a little judgment here. You might not want to broadcast that you're having a highly controversial procedure performed on your anatomy, for example.

4. **Specify when you will return calls.** OK, you're not there, but you're due back soon. What happens then? Let callers know when you'll be returning calls so that they know what to expect.

5. **Offer help—right now.** Some callers may have all the time in the world to wait for the help or guidance they need. Others don't have that luxury. Cover all bases by providing callers with a suggested course of action so that they can get help right away.

6. **Close like a pro.** We've all listened to voicemails that cut off their message rather abruptly, leaving us hanging. Make sure you add a pleasant, professional conclusion to your outgoing message.

You can see how each of these elements helps build a personal, professional outgoing message. Let's put them all together:

"Hello, this is Chris Megargel in Customer Service. Today is January 22nd, and I am out of the office. Please leave a message, and I'll call you back within twenty-four hours. If you need immediate assistance, please press zero to speak with Sheila Baker. Thanks, and have a great day."

A **MAGIC** Moment

Outgoing voicemail messages may seem almost incidental at times. But they can have far-ranging consequences, often when you least expect it. A friend shared the following story:

"One time, the head of the service department at my car dealership left me a message at work and commented on how friendly my voicemail message was.

When I arrived at the dealership, she said she couldn't wait to meet the person with the great message. She then proceeded to give me personal service every time I came in—for years. She called me by name every time and arranged for me to get a loaner car even when it looked like there wasn't one available."

No matter how trivial your communications may seem when you make them, they always have consequences.

Experiment with MAGIC

Now that you have a better feel for what constitutes effective voicemail, go back and re-record your outgoing message. Listen to it again, noting the differences between "before" and "after." Does you new voice message sound more professional? Would you want further contact with that person?

LEAVE PROFESSIONAL MESSAGES

The messages you leave on others' voicemail systems are just as important as your outgoing message. They too should be professional, informative, and thorough.

Think of the messages you've left on other people's voicemails. If you're like most people, they've tended to be one of the following:

- Too casual
- Too curt
- Too long or indirect

We can't say it too often: every bit of communication is an opportunity to make an impression. These brief messages are no exception.

Here are a few step-by-step guidelines:

1. **State your name and when you called.** When you leave a message, be certain to leave your name, the date, and the time of your message. Whether you leave a full name or just a first name depends on the circumstances. If you're contacting a stranger, your full name is more appropriate. Giving only your first name is likely to be OK for a friend or someone else whom you know.

2. **Briefly explain why you're calling.** Many messages are unduly complicated and involved. Provide whatever information you think is important, but keep the message to the point.

3. **Say when it's best to call back.** Your voice message should give the recipient specifics about when and how to get back in touch with you.

4. **Close like a pro.** Don't be any less professional at this end of the conversation than you were in recording an outgoing message.

Let's put these elements together to see an example of a polished incoming message:

"My name is Wendy Morrison, and I'm calling at 3 PM on March first. I'd like more information about your printer options. Please call me at 555-123-4567 until 6 PM. Thanks. I look forward to hearing from you."

Specific content aside, one of the biggest snafus that commonly occur in voice-mail messages is for the caller to sound as though the world will implode if he doesn't finish his message in less than ten seconds. Be sure to take your time. Your message will not only be clearer but also more professional because you're taking adequate time to pass along what's clearly a message of substance.

MAGIC **Maxims**

- Focus on the tone and word choice of your voicemail to make a great impression.
- Make your outgoing voicemail message personal, specific, and informative.
- Leave voicemail messages that are succinct, informative, and professional.

Listening

We can't overstate the importance of listening—careful listening. And by "listening" we don't mean merely the physical process of hearing words. We mean hearing what those words signify. True listening is very much a learned skill—one that goes well beyond bending an ear in someone's direction and looking as though you're engaged.

And listening is one of the key skills in the next MAGIC step: Get to the Heart of the Matter: Listen and Ask Questions.

This step is the transition to the task. The M and A steps of MAGIC were about building and restoring relationship with the customer. Once you've achieved that, then you can proceed to focus on the task. Going to the task too soon creates a transactional environment for you and the customer. It sends the message that the customer is not a person but an "issue" to address or solve. Such an approach can create an overall impression that is routine at best.

THE CHALLENGE OF LISTENING

To really understand and handle the task, you need to listen effectively. If you feel as though your listening skills could stand a bit of polish, don't fret. You've got lots of company.

We have some statistics to illustrate just how challenging effective listening can be. Numerous research studies, among them research on the brain by Roger Sperry, who was awarded the Nobel Prize for medicine in 1981, show that we think faster than we can talk (Sperry, R. W. "Mind-Brain Interaction: Mentalism, Yes; Dualism, No." Reprinted in A. D. Smith, R. Llinas, and P. O. Kostyuk [eds.], *Commentaries in the Neurosciences*. Oxford: Pergamon Press, 1980). We generally speak at a rate of 125 words per minute, but are capable of thinking at 2,000 words per minute.

Imagine: you're hitting on all cylinders, talking away at 125 words a minute, while on the other end my brain is busy churning thoughts at the rate of 2,000 words a minute. Do you think that can make it difficult for me to focus on those paltry few words you're saying? You bet it does!

Research has also indicated that we can really listen to words coming at us slightly in excess of 400 every minute.

Now we've got a real mess on our hands—at least so far as good listening is concerned. You're speaking 125 words every minute, I can handle almost four times as many as that, and, meanwhile, my brain is diverting my attention by pumping out words at some fifteen times the rate you're talking.

What'd you say again?

It's easy to see that solid listening can be a big challenge. The good news is that it is well within our capability—that 400-word-per-minute capacity attests to our inherent potential. It is essential—from the standpoint of empathy and other elements of solid communication—to tap that potential as much as we can.

A **Tragic** Moment

Sometimes people on the phone give the impression that they are merely order takers; you get a kind of "Just tell me what you want, and I'll tell you if we have it or not" feeling (and they won't say anything else; it's just a "yes-no" kind of conversation). These representatives may not have any idea that this is the impression they're making, but customers will respond to it and form a less than positive impression of the company as a whole—and may even take their business elsewhere.

Here's a story from one of our facilitators:

"My husband's boss was very pleased with his performance one year (he won the big account that they always wanted), so he told us that we could go anywhere we wanted for one week. I found a high-end golf vacation company website and saw that they had trips to Lake Como, Italy, which I heard was gorgeous. I called and asked if they had such a trip in October. I explained how excited I was and how anxious to book the vacation of my dreams—after all, the boss was paying for it! I wanted it to be special for my husband since he had won the trip. He's a big golfer and wanted to play on some beautiful yet challenging courses.

"The associate seemed to pay no attention to what I said. Clearly, she regarded me as just another inquiry and responded to me: 'That trip to Italy in October is booked.' She didn't think to tell me of other trips or even to ask me any questions. All I got was a 'no.'

"Clearly, she didn't listen. She didn't seem to hear how significant this was to me (and didn't even hear that the trip was to be an all-expenses-paid vacation!)."

. . . to be continued later in this chapter

THE FOUR LEVELS OF LISTENING

Now that we've established—at least to some degree—that effective listening can be a real challenge, we can move on to discuss some of the particulars that make up listening. More specifically, we want to talk about the four "levels" that comprise people's ability and capacity to listen.

Level One. Here, the dialogue is largely transactional—focused on the task. You recognize what the other person is saying by focusing on facts and details.

Level Two. Rapport building characterizes this level of listening. You ask more questions to gain a greater sense of the other person's meaning.

Level Three. The dialogue is characterized by a sense of warmth and perception. The focus at this level is on empathy. You recognize why the person is speaking and withhold any overriding sense of judgment.

Level Four. This is the deepest level. Your attention is often intuitive, and you remain largely silent. This level is marked by a great deal of patience and tends to promote the sharing of personal meaning.

Much of people's communication—particularly in a business setting—occurs at Levels One and Two. It's largely an empirical process, dominated by an exchange of facts and figures. That's not to say it's "bad"—just, perhaps, not as effective as the level of listening that you would like to establish.

By contrast, Level Four focuses on letting the other person talk and go where she wishes. Typically it only occurs in close relationships where there is trust and mutual respect.

Level Three listening is attentive, nonjudgmental, and genuinely recognizes the other person's feelings and perspective—it is, in a word, empathic. This is the level you want to achieve in your interactions with customers.

HOW TO LISTEN AT LEVEL THREE

However desirable, listening at Level Three is often difficult. You may be preoccupied with other concerns, distracted by what's happening around you, or simply eager to address the problem.

What to do? First, just take a step back and remember that customers are largely the same as you. They work, play, raise their families, pay the cable bill, stay awake at night wondering about the heat versus humidity debate—the whole chimichanga. Occasionally, it's necessary for them to look to others for service and assistance. In so doing, they're relying on those others for help and guidance. When taking a phone call from a client or customer, that's what you're there for.

If you have a tendency to listen at Level One or Two, then you will not "hear" what the customer is really saying. You need to listen to his words and tone in a different way—in a way that goes beyond the facts. Level Three is about listening for and acknowledging the person's feelings and the significance of the issue. Then and only then are you really connecting with the customer and thereby building or restoring the relationship.

So, what do you do when you listen at Level Three? First, listen for the big picture and be careful not to get bogged down in the words and details that are coming at you. Provide a space for the customer to share what's on his mind, without interruption. On the phone, this means listening, letting the customer vent, and responding with phrases that show you "get" what he's going through. In face-to-face interactions, this means maintaining eye contact and an expression of attentiveness, and giving an occasional nod of comprehension.

Now that we've covered your outward behavior, let's move on to what's going on "inside." To be truly empathic, choose a nonjudgmental attitude. Watch your tendencies to make assumptions, judge what you're hearing, or project how you would think or feel in that situation. Just recognize how the person is feeling and accept what she shares.

Level Three listening is distinctly different from what most people tend to do in their customer interactions.

A **MAGIC** Moment

A MAGIC facilitator shared what she learned about herself when she was a participant in the MAGIC program:

"We had just learned about the four levels of listening and were asked to think about how we listen to our friends and business associates. I started by looking at my relationship with my best friend. I could quickly see that he was listening to me at a Level Four. And when I was really honest with myself, I realized that I was only listening to him at a Level Two! I was shocked and thought to myself, 'Am I not a good listener?' But I knew I listened to others at Level Three or even Four. What was happening with my best friend?

"It became clear to me that I talked too much when I was with him; I never gave him time to share this thoughts or concerns. And he must feel drained when he's with me!

"At that point, I made a commitment to change and listen to him at a deeper level. I asked more questions and talked less. I asked him to share more.

"I saw a dramatic difference, and our friendship was stronger than ever. He even said to me, 'You're such a good listener!' And I know that he never would have said that before! It's clear that you can change anything in your communication, if you choose to."

You might be asking, "Why bother with this Level Three stuff?" Valid question— after all, isn't it better to get to the task and move on? Actually, no! We've found that a pure focus on the task leads to increased levels of stress or what is commonly called burnout.

Using Level Three listening will help your calls go more smoothly because your customers will respond to you differently. They will recognize that you care and have the ability and willingness to help. When you choose to listen at Level Three, you influence your customers' perception of you and your ideas. They'll be more receptive and open to collaboration. The end result: shorter calls and less stress.

A **MAGIC** Moment

Remember our facilitator who attempted to book a fabulous golf vacation in Italy? She didn't get anywhere in her encounter with a tragic travel agent who just didn't listen. Well, she made another call to a different agency. Here's what happened:

"I went to the Web and found a different travel service specializing in golf vacations. Instead of being an order taker, this person acted more like a partner, like my personal travel guide or consultant. His first comment was, 'This sounds like the trip of a lifetime. No wonder you're so excited. I have a lot of ideas for you to consider. I'd like to find the best one for you. Could I ask you some questions so I can narrow down the choices?' Finally, I thought to myself, here's someone who really listened!

"He asked me what I wanted to do while I was on the trip, what kinds of hotels I enjoyed, and how much golf I really wanted to play. He also asked about the type of course we prefer and how much we wanted to spend. Once he understood my needs, he came back with some wonderful recommendations. After I expressed interest in a couple of locations, he sent me loads of information to help me make my decision.

"He helped me through the whole process, even recommending that we get car insurance in this foreign country since accidents are common and costly. (Good thing he did—we got a flat tire and were stuck in the middle of nowhere, but since we had insurance, the car rental company came right away to give us a new car.)

"It was a real pleasure to work with him. I even sent him a note after the trip telling him how much we enjoyed it and appreciated his recommendations (and I have never done that before!)."

MAGIC **Maxims**

- Most business communication occurs at Levels One and Two. Level Three listening is rare and thus distinguishes you from other service providers.

- Level Three listening is characterized by attentiveness and a nonjudgmental attitude.

- Empathic listening leads to shorter calls and less stress.

- No one cares how much you know until he knows how much you care.

chapter TWELVE

Get to the Heart

What's the Catchpoint?

S ometimes a customer provides you with too little information, which can make it difficult to determine just what's going on.

But too much information can cause the same problem. It happens all the time when you're dealing with customers on the phone. Often they aren't in the best frame of mind to provide succinct details. Maybe they're upset; perhaps they're just confused. Whatever the reason for the lack of clarity, you often have to wade through a wash of information to get to the heart of the matter.

It's up to you to lead the conversation to uncover what we call the "catchpoint":

- What the caller's issue or need is
- Why that issue is significant to the customer

Put another way, the catchpoint is the "what" and the "why."

Sometimes it's obvious what the customer needs. At other times, her need may be more complex or layered. Often she doesn't tell you up front why that issue is so important to her. For example, she may have received an inaccurate bill. Who hasn't? But this is the fifth time it has happened, and she is fed up and ready to switch providers. She's calling not only to get her bill fixed but also to let you know how angry and upset she is with the whole situation.

But once she knows that you understand her catchpoint, she'll know that you've really listened. She'll feel more secure, knowing that you are really working with her toward a resolution.

If you uncover only *what* the issue is, and not *why* it is significant to the customer, she may feel that you met her need but didn't care about her as an individual. It is important to meet both her task needs and her relational needs.

Here's how to do it.

ASK QUESTIONS TO FIND THE CATCHPOINT

As we mentioned, a caller may be confusing for any number of reasons. She may be angry, upset, or frustrated. She may simply be tired and lacking the energy to adequately explain the issue at hand. She may not even understand her problem herself. (Anyone dealing with the no-man's land of technology, company benefits, or the tax code can certainly empathize with that.) There's a landfill of possible reasons behind a muddled call.

You need to ask probing and clarifying questions to hone in on the real issue:

"What are your specific concerns about your October statement?"

"What are you really looking for in the vacation you're planning?"

"Are you more concerned about the doctor who'll provide your son's care or the medical facility?"

"Tell me exactly what's happening with the product and why it's not working for you."

"Help me understand the impact of the challenge you've had with our services."

REPHRASE AND REPEAT

Many callers ramble from here to there without ever clearly expressing the purpose of their call. Your first step, therefore, is to listen carefully to the caller and then rephrase what you heard. This will show that you are indeed listening and working to understand the situation and need at hand. Here are a few examples of rephrasing:

"So, Max, you're having trouble with your computer. It sounds like you are in a hurry and need to get it fixed before you leave tomorrow. Is that right?"

"Deanna, I'm hearing you say that the bill we sent you appears to be for the second quarter of this year only, and you're looking for a running total that includes the first quarter as well. Did I hear you correctly?"

By rephrasing and then hearing the customer's response, you have an opportunity to confirm or correct your understanding.

Simple repetition is also important. To assure the customer that you have the correct information, it's best for you to repeat back what the customer says. Here's the type of information you'll want to repeat to ensure accuracy:

- Numbers with four or more digits or characters
- New contact information, such as addresses and telephone numbers
- E-mail addresses
- Spelling of names

However, when information is already part of company records, you do not need to repeat it. Simply state to the customer that the information he provided matches the company records.

When it comes to names, even ones that are common, it's always best to double-check. The world is teeming with people named Browne who are probably weary of having the last letter consistently lopped off their name.

Here are some examples:

"I'd like to confirm the spelling of your last name: it was W-I-L-S-H-I-R-E?"

"The serial number was E45019. Is that correct?"

"I can reach you this afternoon at 207-123-4567."

THE "T" WORD

For some callers, the only thing worse than being put on hold is being transferred—the dreaded "T" word. So how do you make them smile when they hear that word? Transfer them with MAGIC, of course. Here's how:

- Lead with a benefit so that the caller understands why it is in his interest to be transferred.
- Ask permission to transfer the call, and wait for a response.
- Give the caller the name and number of the connecting party and note that party's experience or expertise with the matter. This will make the caller more comfortable with the transfer.
- Give the connecting party the caller's name and all relevant information.

- If possible, introduce the caller to the connecting party.
- Close with a MAGIC phrase, such as

  "I'm sure Martin can help you."

  "It was a pleasure speaking with you. All the best with your travel plans."

A **Tragic** Moment

Getting to the heart of the matter is not something that can be scripted. You need to really listen and alter your responses based on what you've heard. A friend shared this story of a rep who focused more on her script than on her customer:

"I called a large computer manufacturer about a problem with one of their products. The person who answered asked what was wrong, and I proceeded to tell her. I explained the issue very clearly and slowly so that she could help me quickly. She then proceeded to ask five or six more questions—most of which I had just answered. Clearly she wasn't listening at all to me, just asking questions on a script. When I told her that I had already answered some of the questions, she said that she 'had to ask the questions; it was her job.'

"When I asked if there was someone else there who could help me, she said she would transfer me to a supervisor. Before transferring me, she asked the question I suppose she must ask on the script before ending any call: 'Is there anything else I can do for you?' I simply said no, since she hadn't done much of anything for me at all."

WHY ASK QUESTIONS?

Posing clarifying questions, probing for more information, and repeating key things you have heard accomplish several important objectives:

- You're more likely to grasp the "what" and the "why."
- You're more likely to satisfy the customer's needs.
- You're more likely to control the conversation in a professional fashion.
- You make a better impression on the customer.
- You save time.

An example will help you appreciate the subtleties of this process and illustrate the skills involved in steps M through G. Say you take a call from a Mr. Adams. He is, to put it mildly, livid. He spews out a series of threats and says, "What's wrong with you people? Why haven't I gotten my order? I need it now!"

You listen without interrupting. Then, once you do have a chance to politely interrupt, you begin to build some bridges:

1. **Express empathy.**

   "Mr. Adams, I understand the urgency, and I will help right now."

2. **Ask permission.** Now move on to asking pertinent questions. If you need to ask two or more, ask permission. This helps put the caller at ease, shows that you are genuinely interested, and helps you establish control of the situation in a professional manner.

   "Mr. Adams, to help you quickly, I will need to ask a few questions. Is that OK?"

3. **Ask probing and clarifying questions.** Now's the time to get at the heart of what has made Mr. Adams so upset. You do this by asking questions that both probe and clarify the issue. From there, ask questions to confirm that those are, in fact, the central issues.

   "Mr. Adams, what did you order, and when did you expect to receive it?"

4. **Rephrase and repeat.** By now, your questioning has clearly identified the real issue. Restate that conclusion for the caller so that he knows you understand.

   "I see. Your son's twenty-first birthday is tomorrow, and you want to be sure that the gift gets there in time for this important event. You're concerned that the gift may be late, and you're upset about not getting the responses you need. I'd be happy to take care of this to put your mind at ease."

At this point, you've zeroed in on the catchpoint.

The "what" is that the item has not arrived. The "why" is that he's concerned that the gift won't arrive in time and that the company has not given him any reassurance whatsoever.

Depending on what Mr. Adams was saying at the outset of the conversation, it may have been a real challenge to pinpoint these issues. Now, armed with the knowledge of the real problem, you can set to work addressing it, such as by arranging for overnight shipping of the item free of charge so that it's sure to arrive in time for the birthday.

But you've done more than just arrange for a package to go out overnight. By expressing empathy with the caller, by acting professionally and moving the conversation forward in the most constructive manner possible, you have established a real connection with that caller—one that not only works toward a solution but does so in a way that the customer will likely remember.

A **Tragic** Moment

A MAGIC program participant told us this story about a fellow representative who couldn't understand why a customer was so angry and upset. It's clear that this rep didn't get the customer's catchpoint.

"A frustrated customer called our catalogue company inquiring about the clothing she had ordered for her college-bound son. He was going from a very warm climate to a cold climate, so she wanted him to be prepared with warm clothes.

"She was very upset that many of the items she bought were back-ordered. And she was annoyed about getting notices of delays on the few items that were available.

"Frustrated, she called the company. She became very emotional, saying she couldn't understand why the company couldn't deliver a pair of socks pictured in its catalogue.

"What with her anger, the call went on for a while. When she finally finished, the rep who handled her call threw up his hands and exclaimed, 'Can you believe it? All over a lousy pair of socks!'

"After hearing about this story from the rep, it was clear to me that it wasn't just the socks. It had to do with frustration with the fact that this was yet another item that was inexplicably back-ordered, not to mention concern for her son going off to a cold climate without being properly outfitted. If the rep had understood the catchpoint of the conversation, the call could have ended very differently.

"It's unlikely that this customer will order from our company ever again."

LET ME PUT YOU ON HOLD . . .

"Hold on. . ."

"Hang on a sec. . ."

"Hold please. . ."

"Mind if I put you on hold?"

"I'm going to have to put you on hold."

Who hasn't heard these dreaded words? Putting callers on hold may be a typical part of your interactions, yet you may not have given a lot of thought to the way you choose to do it. If you tend to use one of the examples we just gave, we have news for you. They're tragic! Here's why: the overall impression is that they're sloppy and far too casual. The caller may be thinking, "Do I even have a choice here?" or "What's in it for me?" or "Yeah, I *do* mind." The bottom line is that these phrases are more about you than about the customer.

So how do you put someone on hold in a MAGIC way? Use the following steps:

1. Explain the reason you need to place the caller on hold—lead with a benefit.

2. Ask permission to put the caller on hold, and wait for a response.

3. After the hold, say the caller's name and thank him for holding.

Here's how it might sound:

"I need to look up your account so that I can give you an accurate balance. Are you able to hold while I do that?" (*You put the caller on hold, then get back on the line.*)

"Ms. Juarez, thank you for holding. I have that information for you now."

Note that we suggest you say the customer's name right when you come back from the hold. By using her name first, you prepare her to listen. After all, she may have become preoccupied with other thoughts or activities while on hold. Customers use that downtime to check their e-mail or the pot on the stove.

MAGIC **Maxims**

- Be aware that a customer's real issue may not be readily apparent at first.

- To help uncover a customer's catchpoint, empathize and ask questions to understand the "what" and the "why."

- Rephrase and repeat key points to confirm their importance and establish a basis for a constructive solution.

- Understand that uncovering the real issue—and why it's significant to the caller—will help you come to a resolution more quickly and efficiently.

Moving On

chapter
THIRTEEN

W e've addressed the first three steps: Make a Connection, Act Professionally, and Get to the Heart of the Matter (the catchpoint).

Now it's time for the I in MAGIC: Inform and Clarify What You Will Do.

You've learned how to gain the customer's respect and trust by connecting, listening, and empathizing. You've also demonstrated professionalism and learned how to uncover the customer's catchpoint—not just what she is calling about but also why the issue matters to her.

Now you shift from listening and understanding to taking action. Here is where you demonstrate a commitment to work with, not against, the customer.

BE PROACTIVE: OFFER OPTIONS AND SOLUTIONS

Now's the time to begin to work with all you've heard during the call—to offer solutions. As you might imagine, this is a turning point in the conversation. After all, isn't this why the caller picked up the phone in the first place—to have a problem or issue addressed in some manner?

The key is for you to lead the interaction and offer options before the customer asks. If he offers solutions first, he may suggest ideas you simply cannot implement. If you offer solutions first, you take the lead and offer solutions you know you can act on.

Here are some examples:

"To expedite this process, I can e-mail you the documents in a PDF format."

"To avoid this in the future, I would be happy to send you a reminder at the first of each month."

103

"Have you given any thought to the optional rider? That would offer the additional protection you're interested in. I would be happy to send you complete information on that product."

"You may wish to consider buying extra printer cartridges now so that you have them for your big production run. Would that be helpful?"

Notice what these solutions have in common. First, they're all proactive—you're actively offering to do something for the caller without waiting to be asked. Second, they are all personal and specific; in each case, you are addressing the caller's needs in a highly detailed fashion—for example, by mentioning PDF format or specifically targeting the first of every month. Third, you're demonstrating responsibility by identifying a specific and actionable solution or alternative.

SET A DEADLINE

Your emphasis on specificity should apply as much to *when* you intend to do something as *what* you intend to do. Setting deadlines is a critical follow-up to your proposed solutions.

Don't wait for the customer to ask when the information or package she requested might arrive. Instead, propose a deadline you know you can meet.

Deadlines, however, come in a greater variety than they might seem to at first glance. For instance:

"I will e-mail you an update by 2 PM Friday."

"I have entered the updated information into your file. The changes will take effect by the end of business today."

"Your application is done. It will take no more than three days to complete the review process."

As you can see, deadlines set a time frame, but in different ways. In every case, however, they establish a certainty. Like other steps in this process, deadlines are specific and actionable.

Ever been through something like this at a car dealership?

Your car has a mechanical problem. You arrive at the dealership, and the friendly service manager walks you through paperwork and questions. Here's how that scenario can finish up:

Service: OK, have a seat, and we'll call you when it's ready.

You: When will that be?

Service: Gee, I really don't know. We're down a mechanic today, and I'm not sure just what we'll have to do until we get it up on the lift.

You: You don't have any idea at all? I have to get to work!

Service: Well. We're doing the best we can.

You *(with a heavy sigh):* Right . . .

Why wouldn't the service manager have an answer to that question? Doesn't everyone who comes in ask pretty much the same thing? Couldn't he have been proactive and set a deadline?

Let's rework that scenario with a focus on being proactive and setting reasonable deadlines:

Service: OK, I have all the info I need. I bet you'd like to know when your car might be ready.

You: Certainly.

Service: We're down a mechanic, and I really won't know the extent of the issue until we get it up on a lift. I'd be happy to give you an update in thirty or forty minutes.

You: Thanks. How long will it take, because I really have to get to work . . .

Service: I understand you're in a hurry. What I can do is get back to you in thirty minutes with an estimated completion time.

You: OK, that works. Thanks!

EDUCATE THE CUSTOMER

During the course of a call, there are various ways you can educate your customer. This can help her understand

- Your processes and time frames
- Your range of products and services
- Options or alternatives that might be of benefit to her

Customers also get a sense of added value when you share this type of information. Think about it: your goal is to handle each contact so appropriately that the customer chooses to contact you again. To this end, educating your customers will serve to further differentiate you from competitors. Customers remember these sorts of experiences.

When a rep is encouraged to give guidance and advice to customers, he effectively becomes a "subject-matter expert" in those customers' eyes. Further, he feels a greater sense of pride and contribution in his role within your organization.

A **MAGIC** Moment

Using similes, metaphors, and analogies can prove effective in educating customers. One of our contacts at an auto financing business unit of a large New York bank shared this story:

"Julie Williams called to find out if the customer—an elderly woman—was going to return the leased car or buy it. Within a few minutes, it was clear that the customer thought there was a scam going on. She repeated that she had been making monthly payments and that the car would be 'paid off' within a short time.

"After a few clarifying questions, Julie realized that the woman simply didn't understand what a lease agreement was. Her husband had recently passed away, and he had been the one who had always handled the finances. Julie explained, 'Ms. Perez, a lease is like borrowing a book from the library. You have possession of it and the right to use it, but you don't own it. You've been paying for use of the car, but you don't own it.'

"At that point, there was a long pause. It was clear that Julie had helped Ms. Perez understand the idea of leasing by drawing an analogy with a concept that Ms. Perez understood."

SUMMARIZE THE NEXT STEP

Having offered a solution as well as a deadline (not to mention some education), follow through on the specifics by telling the caller what he likely wants to know: what exactly is going to happen next. For example:

"I will contact our technical support staff this morning to arrange an on-site call. I will let you know by the end of the day when that will take place."

"The manager is out on an appointment now, but I will speak with her the minute she gets back. You can expect a call from her by 4 PM today Eastern time."

"You will send in your rebate forms. Once I have them in hand, I'll expedite their processing."

By summarizing the actions to be taken, you're repeating the next step to the customer. That way, you both understand what is supposed to happen next. Make sure you're both clear on any responsibilities either of you may have. Doing so reduces the chances of any misunderstandings. Summarizing also offers additional security that whatever steps need to be taken will in fact be taken.

GET AGREEMENT ON THE NEXT STEP

Now that you've offered a next step, it's important to ensure that the caller agrees with that next step.

You can get that agreement in a number of ways. For instance, you may phrase a suggested next step in the following manner:

"Mr. Jones, I will contact customer service and get back to you by noon today. How does that sound?"

"Ms. Johannsen, I'll notify Janet of your call the moment she is off her conference call so she can get back with you. Will you be there for the next hour?"

The point here is to specify the action you intend to take and to actively solicit a response from the caller—one that helps you know that she heard what you said and agrees with that course of action.

Make certain that the caller's agreement is positive. You should expect a clear expression of willingness on his part. That means you're looking for such responses as "Yes, that sounds good to me" or "That would be fine." What you don't want to hear are such answers as "I guess so," "If that's the best you can do," or other phrases that express disappointment or reluctance.

If you hear one of these, consider one of the following strategies:

- Explore other options and time frames as alternatives.

- Restate the next step you've presented, outlining why you think it's appropriate and how it will benefit the customer.

- Hear the customer out. Let him explain what he thinks the next step should be. Restate what you heard him say. From there, you can accept that alternative or, if you cannot, empathize with the caller and explain why his idea does not work and what you can do.

By soliciting and receiving confirmation on the next step, you ensure that you and the caller are on the same page. You both know what has happened up to this point, and you both know what is going to happen next. Through these simple actions, you minimize the likelihood of any sort of miscommunication or confusion ("I never agreed to that!").

MAGIC **Maxims**

- As you near the end of a call, be proactive by offering solutions and alternatives.

- Take the initiative to identify options or information that may benefit the caller. The customer will appreciate it, and you'll feel good about the added value you've provided.

- Don't wait for customers to ask questions about timing. Set deadlines that you know you can meet.

- Before closing the call, summarize and get agreement on the next step.

Close with the Relationship in Mind

At this point, you're ready for the final step—the C in MAGIC: Close with the Relationship in Mind.

Your closing is the final impression a caller will have of both you and the organization you represent. It's what she's going to take away. We all tend to remember our very last bit of contact with someone else. If it was great, it reinforces everything else that was positive about the encounter. If it was less than great or even unpleasant, we're not sure we want to have any further contact with that person.

Closing a conversation is as important as every other element that preceded it, and there are specific skills to use to ensure a lasting great impression.

MAKE A LAST OFFER OF HELP

How many times have you found yourself as a customer saying, "Hold on, I have another question!" or "I'm not done yet!"

Your customer won't need to jump in if you offer him the opportunity to raise additional issues or ask final questions—even to address something that's been covered already.

To do that in the best way possible, use a MAGIC phrase and ask the caller if there's anything further she wishes to discuss. For instance:

"What else may I help you with today?"

"What other questions do you have?"

"Is there anything else I can help you with today?"

A word to the wise: avoid sounding as though you're asking the question out of a sense of obligation—as though it were part of a script from which you don't dare deviate. If your question sounds scripted, it's going to sound insincere.

Just as important, you need to consider when it's appropriate to ask if there's anything else you can do. That may not be the right thing to ask if

- You transferred the call to someone else.
- You were unable to answer the caller's questions or otherwise help her, for whatever reason.

However, in most situations, your question extends the courtesy of service.

USE THE CUSTOMER'S NAME AND A MAGIC PHRASE

Before ending the call, it's important to use the customer's name. It's very much like a handshake at the end of a face-to-face meeting.

Using the caller's name helps her feel important and strengthens the relationship. If it's one of the last things she hears, it will reinforce her feeling that she received truly personal service.

Every moment in contact with a customer is an opportunity to make a great impression. Seize that moment and use a MAGIC phrase at the conclusion of a call. By that, we don't mean some bland "Thank you" or "You're welcome," which can take very little effort. That's hardly exceptional. Instead, both the words and the tone with which you deliver those words need to be sincere. Here are some worthy candidates for your consideration:

"Thanks so much for calling, Mr. Roberts. Have a terrific day."

"I appreciate your letting me know about this, Mr. Mattes. Thanks again for calling, and enjoy the rest of your afternoon."

You can also step it up a notch and offer your name and express a willingness to help in the future, when it's appropriate. For instance:

"If you have any other questions on this topic, feel free to contact me directly. My name is Marie, and you can reach me at 417-245-6750."

Again, a MAGIC phrase seals the conversation in a positive, upbeat, sincere, and impeccably professional fashion. And that one final use of the name reinforces the customer's sense of having received highly personal attention.

STAY WITH THE CUSTOMER TO THE END

We've all endured the experience of someone hanging up on us. It's not pleasant in the least; the hollow finality of that click at the other end of the line is, if nothing else, abrupt and awkward.

Don't undo all you've built by inadvertently ending the call in that manner—what we refer to as the "slam dunk." Hanging up first can make the caller feel as though he were rushed off the phone whether he was ready or not. You never want to give a caller the impression that he didn't have all the time he needed to cover what he had to discuss in sufficient detail.

Also pay attention to the possibility of a "fade-away"—in its own fashion, just as ineffective a way to wrap up a conversation. In this case, you mumble goodbye or, even worse, fail to say goodbye at all. Although this isn't as abrupt as a slam dunk, it's no less awkward. If nothing else, it can leave a caller wondering whether the conversation is, in fact, finished or not.

Both the slam dunk and the fade-away can be avoided by using a MAGIC phrase to conclude the conversation and giving the caller the chance to hang up the line first. When she hangs up, it's clear that she's done and has no further questions.

FOLLOW THROUGH

Now that you've completed your call, your task is to follow through on the commitments you made in your conversation. By using MAGIC steps during the call, you gain the customer's confidence. By following through, you keep it.

Here are some suggestions and strategies to help you keep that commitment:

- Review your notes. Highlight any particularly critical points, important pieces of information, or actionable steps.
- Identify what you and the caller agreed would happen next.
- Note the time frame of next steps.
- Set your schedule accordingly.
- Keep the caller informed as necessary.
- Let the caller know if any problems arise.
- Keep the caller informed if things move faster than anticipated.
- Remain proactive.

- Look for opportunities for additional service. You already know what you need to do. Now's your chance to exceed expectations and really stand out— to go beyond the ordinary to the extraordinary. If, for example, you told a caller that a shipment would be on its way by Friday, see if Thursday or even earlier might be possible. If you said you'd call back by day's end, target midday to touch base and pleasantly surprise the caller with your efficiency. Perhaps you can make a small gesture of kindness, such as by sending a thank-you note and a free sample, or a more involved one (see, for example, the next MAGIC Moment). The possibilities are endless!

A **MAGIC** Moment

Here's an anecdote from a friend who found a retail site on the Web that wowed her with above-and-beyond service:

"I came across these cool book clips while searching the Internet. I decided to order six as stocking stuffers for my family.

"I hadn't given it another thought until I received a personal e-mail—from the vendor herself:

"'Hello Devon. Thank you for your order. We shipped it last week, but it came back today because the address label came off in the mail. I could tell it was you by your specific color choices. We will mail your order out again tomorrow and you'll have them by the end of next week. I'm sorry for the delay but am glad I was able to sort out the orders and find it was yours that was returned. I'm including an extra clip as an apology for the delay. Best regards, Florence.'

"Wow! She could have shipped those book clips off without so much as a word to me. I never would have known. But she chose to figure out that it was my order, inform me of the delay, repack it, apologize, and throw in a free extra clip!"

MAGIC **Maxims**

- When appropriate, be sure to extend the offer of additional help at the end of a call.
- In closing the call, maintain the connection with the caller by using her name and a MAGIC phrase.
- Do what you say you will do—and look for opportunities to go beyond what you promise.

Assess Your Calls with MAGIC

T he telephone call is over. Now your work is just beginning. How do you know if you made a great impression on the caller? Let's find out.

PUTTING IT ALL TOGETHER: WHAT IMPRESSION DO YOU MAKE?

As of this point in the book we have covered all of the MAGIC skills and steps. Now it's time to talk about them as one cogent whole.

Exhibit 15.1 is a list of The 33 Points of MAGIC for incoming calls, the best practice behaviors that are part of The Five MAGIC Steps. These best practices can become the standard of contact quality in your organization, and you can use them to assess your calls and the impression you make on customers.

Exhibit 15.1: The 33 Points of MAGIC—Incoming Calls

Make a Connection: Build the Relationship

1. Greeting: Offer welcoming words.
2. Greeting: Maintain an upbeat tone.
3. Greeting: Use an unhurried pace.
4. Listen and don't interrupt.
5. Express empathy through words.
6. Express empathy through tone.
7. Use the customer's name as soon as you hear it.
8. Tell the customer you will help.
9. Ask permission to gain more information.

Exhibit 15.1: The 33 Points of MAGIC—Incoming Calls, Cont'd.

Act Professionally: Express Confidence

10. Express sincerity and helpfulness through tone.
11. Maintain an appropriate pace.
12. Speak clearly with proper volume.
13. Use "I," not "we," when appropriate.
14. Use "please" and "thank you" to show courtesy.
15. Avoid tragic phrases and jargon.
16. Use MAGIC phrases to build confidence and trust.

Get to the Heart of the Matter: Listen and Ask Questions

17. Ask questions to find the catchpoint (the "what" and the "why").
18. Listen and rephrase appropriately.
19. Repeat numbers (four or more) and new contact information.
20. Before a hold or transfer, explain why and get permission.
21. After a hold: Use the customer's name, wait for a response, and thank him or her.
22. Keep the interaction to an appropriate length.

Inform and Clarify What You Will Do

23. Be proactive: Offer options or solutions.
24. Set a deadline or time frame before the customer asks.
25. Educate with relevant information.
26. Be knowledgeable and accurate.
27. Summarize the next step(s).
28. Get the customer's agreement on the next step(s).

Close with the Relationship in Mind

29. Offer additional assistance when appropriate.
30. Use the customer's name.
31. End with a MAGIC phrase.
32. Close with a sincere tone.
33. Did you lead the interaction closer to resolution?

Let's go back to where we started: MAGIC—the acronym for **Make A Great Impression on the Customer**. Making a great impression is, after all, the purpose of The 33 Points. And, you can use this list to assess the quality of your customer interactions.

You're probably wondering how your "score" on The 33 Points relates to the impression you make. Our research with clients over the last twenty-five years has shown a connection between the MAGIC assessment and customer perception:

Your Score:	Impression You Make:
1–18	Discouraging
19–22	Indifferent
23–25	Routine
26–28	Very good
29–33	Exceptional

Most organizations score 25 at best on The 33 Points, which is why service is so ho-hum in most of people's experience. In fact, as Figure 15.1 illustrates, if your team or organization scores 25 or less, then your culture could be costing you money! How so? Think of the impact of less than great service: you can lose customers, receive fewer repeat purchases, and fewer referrals.

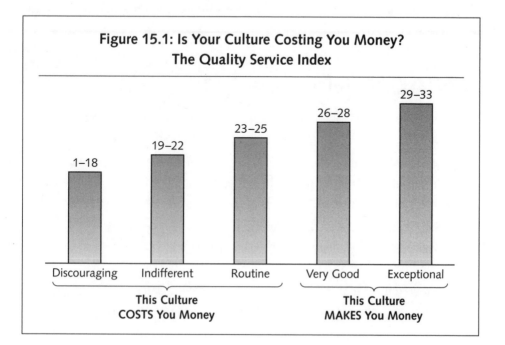

Figure 15.1: Is Your Culture Costing You Money?
The Quality Service Index

If your team or organization as a whole embraces and practices MAGIC, you can create a culture that *makes* you money because customers will continue to buy from you, buy more of the same products from you and potentially buy other products you offer, and refer you to others. We talk more about creating a culture of above-and-beyond service in Chapter Seventeen.

The good news is that you now know the skills needed to make an exceptional impression and create a MAGIC culture. If you make the choice to learn and practice them, you are well on the way to making a consistently professional impression.

We know that The 33 Points may seem like a lot of skills to master. But remember that you're probably doing a lot of them already. To set yourself apart and raise the bar, focus on mastering the details. Think of one of your favorite recipes that you make on special occasions—one that requires a lot of ingredients and effort, but is really worth it. Now imagine if you cut corners and leave out two or three ingredients. Is it likely to taste the same and get your usual rave reviews? Probably not. Consider a musical performance. If the guitarist is a no-show, the piece will sound completely different—which may not be a good thing. Clearly, it's the little things that make the difference, whether it's an ingredient in a favorite dish, an instrument in a musical piece, or an element of an interaction.

By focusing on the details of your interactions, you'll start to notice that people will respond differently. You may also find that you'll feel better too. With MAGIC, everyone benefits.

A **MAGIC** Moment

Sometimes a MAGIC Moment can stretch into a marathon, depending on the complexity of the situation. A friend recorded this shining example:

"I was delighted that my company had just given me a brand-new laptop. The computer and I were getting along just fine until I tried to hook up to the Internet at home. I tried everything I knew, then called our help desk provider.

"Luckily, I got Jason. We started talking at about 9 in the morning; our final chat was at about 7:40 that evening. If you've ever taken the express to techno hell, this was it!

"Jason walked me through every possibility before arriving at that Eureka moment that unraveled the whole mystery. When I used phrases like 'wire-thingy,'

Jason patiently asked me to describe it for him. When I insisted there was no power source, Jason stayed on the line while I crawled under the desk to sort through a scramble of cords and wires.

"And when I had to rummage through old documentation that might offer some clues, Jason stayed on the line. He even drove to the office where my old laptop was to see if any helpful information might be there. Nothing was too much time, trouble, or effort for him.

"We may have been seventy-seven miles apart, but Jason was right there with me. His patience and humor were matched by his problem-solving skills and ability to translate tech-speak into everyday English.

"Our marathon left me up and running, perfectly connected. But Jason wasn't done: he wrote documentation for others in the support team in the event I called in again. And, after I had mentioned in passing that I would love a screensaver with peacock feathers, he even e-mailed several terrific pictures for my consideration.

"Talk about exceptional service! I'll be telling this story for a long time to come. Thank you, thank you, Jason."

MAGIC—IT'S NOT JUST A CHECKLIST

Despite the lineup of The 33 Points we just presented, it's important to remember that MAGIC is not a mere checklist. It's a process of interaction that focuses both on relationships and on the tasks you need to accomplish. Instead of thinking, "All I need to do is check off each item on the checklist," recognize that The 33 Points are a set of behaviors that work together to make a great impression on a customer. As behaviors, they are skills you can learn, develop, and eventually master so that they become natural, authentic, and automatic.

When you use these skills, you express respect for the other person and demonstrate professionalism and accountability. So it is not just about "doing" MAGIC; it is also about "being" MAGIC and bringing these behaviors and this mind-set to every interaction.

It's also important to note that The 33 Points can be customized to specific environments so that they are aligned with an organization's needs. For example, you may want to emphasize cross-selling or up-selling. These skills can be integrated into The 33 Points to reflect those goals.

Experiment with MAGIC

Pair up with a colleague or coworker. Come up with some typically challenging incoming customer calls. Make them interesting and realistic—difficult but not relentless.

Have one person take on the role of the customer; the other, the company representative. Act out a scenario, with the representative using The 33 Points as a guide. See how many of The 33 Points you can use—notice the impact on the "customer" and on his responses.

As you debrief, consider the following questions:

- What did you notice overall?
- What impression did the representative convey?
- Did the rep control the call professionally?
- Is the customer closer to a resolution?
- What MAGIC or tragic phrases did you hear?

As you review, focus on specific steps in the overall process, adding ones you may have overlooked and polishing those already in place. To give yourself a different perspective, record your practice. Then play it back and use The 33 Points to assess the interaction.

Once you are done, reverse roles and repeat the exercise with a brand-new scenario.

OUTGOING CALLS

Outgoing calls are somewhat different from incoming; if nothing else, you're the one who's placing the call. That raises several distinct issues that warrant some attention.

Preparing to Make Your Outgoing Call

Before you make an outgoing call, it's important to prepare. Here are some guidelines:

- Gather any information you may need for the call. Have it organized and accessible.

- Bear in mind the other person's communication style and prepare to accommodate it. For instance, some people want to get straight down to business, whereas others prefer to chat a bit. Prepare yourself to match those style preferences.

- Know your questions. List every question you may need to ask. That way, you can be as efficient and productive as possible.

- Anticipate the other person's questions. Prepare a set of answers for questions you expect.

Opening Your Outgoing Call

There are specific, effective ways to begin an outgoing call:

- First, identify yourself and the company or organization you represent.

- Let the other person know up front about any benefit he may receive as a result of your call. For instance, you may have news or other important information he's been waiting to hear. Push that good news up toward the top of your list.

- Make sure it's a convenient time for the other person to receive the call. All the good news in the world may lose its impact if now's not a good time for the other person to talk. Ask her if it is; if it isn't, find out when it would be more convenient.

Put these elements together, and you get something like this:

"Hi, Bill, this is Veronica from Smith Associates. I have those projections we've been putting together for you. Is now a good time to review them?"

"Hello, Dawn, this is Brad from Kimball Inc. calling. I'm returning your call regarding the invoices. Is this a convenient time for us to go over those?"

The 33 Points of MAGIC for Outgoing Calls

As for incoming calls, there are 33 Points of MAGIC for outgoing calls. They're listed in Exhibit 15.2, and we've italicized the points that are different for outgoing as opposed to incoming calls.

Exhibit 15.2: The 33 Points of MAGIC—Outgoing Calls

Make a Connection: Build the Relationship

1. Greeting: Offer welcoming words.
2. Greeting: Maintain an upbeat tone.
3. Greeting: Use an unhurried pace.
4. *Use the customer's name.*
5. *Tell the customer how he or she will benefit from the call.*
6. *Ensure that the customer is available to speak.*
7. *Give the big picture; ask permission to gain more information.*
8. *Express empathy through words.*
9. *Express empathy through tone.*

Act Professionally: Express Confidence

10. Express sincerity and helpfulness through tone.
11. Maintain an appropriate pace.
12. Speak clearly with proper volume.
13. Use "I," not "we," when appropriate.
14. Use "please" and "thank you" to show courtesy.
15. Avoid tragic phrases and jargon.
16. Use MAGIC phrases to build confidence and trust.

Get to the Heart of the Matter: Listen and Ask Questions

17. Ask questions to find the catchpoint (the "what" and the "why").
18. Listen and rephrase appropriately.
19. Repeat numbers (four or more) and new contact information.
20. Before a hold or transfer, explain why and get permission.
21. After a hold: Use the customer's name, wait for response, and thank him or her.
22. Keep the interaction to an appropriate length.

Inform and Clarify What You Will Do

23. Be proactive: Offer options or solutions.

24. Set a deadline or time frame before the customer asks.

25. Educate with relevant information.

26. Be knowledgeable and accurate.

27. Summarize the next step(s).

28. Get the customer's agreement on the next step(s).

Close with the Relationship in Mind

29. Offer additional assistance when appropriate.

30. Use the customer's name.

31. End with a MAGIC phrase.

32. Close with a sincere tone.

33. Did you lead the interaction closer to resolution?

Experiment with MAGIC

Practice outgoing calls as you would incoming calls. Work with a colleague and role-play an outgoing call. Keep an eye on The 33 Points as you proceed through the call. As you did with incoming calls, pay attention not only to each of The 33 Points but also note the impact the points have on the conversation.

When you debrief, ask yourself the same questions with which you concluded your incoming call exercise:

- What did you notice overall?
- What impression did the representative convey?
- Did the rep control the call professionally?
- Is the customer closer to a resolution?
- What MAGIC or tragic phrases did you hear?

TAKE IT STEP-BY-STEP

Whether you do so through a formal exercise or not, it's always helpful to keep The 33 Points in mind in any conversation. Just think of the five-step framework, which provides a logical progression:

Make a Connection: Build the Relationship

Act Professionally: Express Confidence

Get to the Heart of the Matter: Listen and Ask Questions

Inform and Clarify What You Will Do

Close with the Relationship in Mind

To help you achieve a new level of communication and caller satisfaction with each and every call, focus on two or three skills in each step. Then gradually add more as time goes on. Soon you'll find that your interactions have improved and you're using the skills more naturally.

MAGIC **Maxims**

- The 33 Points of MAGIC will help you lead any conversation with professionalism and grace.
- The 33 Points take you step-by-step through each call, emphasizing empathy, connection, and accountability.
- You can use The 33 Points both to practice calls and to review calls after you're done to see the impact these skills can make.
- MAGIC points become MAGIC skills with practice.

chapter SIXTEEN

Handling Complaints and Difficult Situations

I n this chapter, we address a variety of challenging scenarios and how to handle them so that instead of dreading them, you'll face them with a feeling of confidence.

THE JOY OF COMPLAINT

Strangely enough, someone who complains can often prove to be one of the most valuable people you need to listen to. Consider these statistics from TARP (*Basic Facts on Customer Complaint Behavior and the Impact of Service on the Bottom Line,* 1999, and *Using Complaints for Quality Assurance Decisions,* 1997. Arlington, Va.: TARP Worldwide U.S.):

- Only 4 percent of dissatisfied customers actually complain. (The lion's share—the remaining 96 percent—merely leave.) Moreover, six out of every ten of those dissatisfied people have genuinely serious concerns.

- From there, the bad news spreads: dissatisfied customers tell an average of ten people about their negative experience.

There is, however, an upside to working with a customer with a bona fide complaint:

- Merely listening to a complaint boosts your chances of retaining that customer.

- People who complain and are satisfied are up to 8 percent more loyal than if they had no problem at all.

- Some 95 percent of complainants who are quickly satisfied remain loyal.

Clearly, a complaining customer offers an opportunity to build the relationship and the bottom line.

HOT BUTTONS AND SELF-MANAGEMENT

When people are in the heart of difficult situations, they tend to react emotionally. It's perfectly natural: rather than really thinking about how to respond to a difficult person or situation, most people just let their emotions take them where they will.

Natural, yes, but not particularly effective. And emotional reactions often don't lend themselves to a positive outcome.

That's particularly true in difficult situations, no matter if they involve a customer with a complaint or someone who crosses the line into anger or abuse.

To handle difficult situations effectively, you need to go beyond your natural reactions. This is what we mean by *self-management.* Implicit in this term is the idea that, in many ways, difficult situations are really more about you than they are the other person. Self-management means focusing on what you can control and influence—once again, we're talking about your locus of control. In this sense, managing difficult situations comes down to dealing with what's really going on inside you and how you react to different situations and circumstances; it comes down to understanding your "hot buttons"—the things that trigger strong emotional reactions within you.

Hot buttons come in all forms, and they differ from one person to another. What's "hot" to one person may be decidedly cool to another. For some of us, it can be a particular word or phrase that angers or irritates us. Sometimes, it's body language, tone, a belief or opinion, or some other element that just seems to hit home on an emotional level. But no matter the trigger, hot buttons can be very powerful.

Experiment with MAGIC

The first step to managing your hot buttons is to identify them. Take a few minutes to list some of yours. What sorts of things—spoken and otherwise—really catch you squarely between the eyes and, more often than not, draw forth a powerful emotional response? Here are a few examples to get you thinking:

- Someone rolling her eyes
- Demanding words and tone
- Condescending manner
- Someone snapping at you
- Someone blaming you
- Someone who insists on speaking to a supervisor
- Someone who needs extensive help and hand holding
- Someone who tells you his life story

Now think in particular about the hot buttons pushed by clients or customers. How do you react to these hot buttons? Do you become angry, upset, worried, sad, defensive, or frustrated, or do you have another reaction?

It's important to understand that your hot buttons and reactions are personal patterns that you have adopted over time and that, in effect, have become habits.

The good news is that you can change your responses and thereby your habits. Think about it: your responses to hot buttons involve choice. No one "makes" you respond in a certain fashion. Rather, you have learned how to react, and you choose to do so.

Continuing to react emotionally to your hot buttons in difficult situations can have long-term implications for both you and your relationships with others. Customers may not just be dissatisfied; they may never return.

Experiment with MAGIC

Let's approach our discussion of hot buttons from a slightly different perspective. This time, think about hot buttons that no longer elicit a strong response from you—that are in effect no longer hot buttons. If you need a bit of guidance, think back to your younger years (we'll let you decide what those are!). Chances are good that there are things to which you no longer respond in a particularly powerful or emotional way; in other words, there were a few hot buttons in your past that no longer have the powerful connection they once had.

This exercise can help you realize that how you reacted in the past simply wasn't effective. Perhaps you chose to see the situation differently and, therefore, chose a different response. The key point to remember is that every hot button is an opportunity to explore your thoughts and rethink a response.

CHANGING YOUR RESPONSES

Those hot buttons that are no longer hot buttons illustrate your capacity to change—specifically, your capacity to change your response to all sorts of things, including the most maddening hot buttons imaginable. The truth is beyond debate: it may not be easy or simple to do, but you *can* change your responses.

Now review the hot buttons you listed in the first Experiment with MAGIC. Bearing in mind your capacity for change, what do you think you can do to see those situations in a different light and make different choices—to effectively defuse those hot buttons?

We'll describe one strategy that can help, but first we need to give you a little background. When you're on the job—the front lines, if you will—difficult situations can make you feel as though you're stuck or being attacked or cornered. Again, such feelings are perfectly natural—for example, when you're dealing with a caller complaining about a lost shipment or, worse, somehow or other blaming you for the foibles of the shipping company, it's all too easy to feel that he has you trapped between a rock and a hard place.

When people feel they are under attack, they often experience that perceived attack in a physical way. You've no doubt heard of it: the fight-or-flight response. Their heart pounds, their muscles tense up, and their palms may feel sweaty. These physical signals are followed by a psychological reaction. In difficult interactions with customers, this reaction tends to take one of three forms:

Fight: Rather than simply "taking it," you fight back by defending yourself, claiming it's not your fault, or perhaps shifting blame to the customer.

Flight: This is an emotional "exit, stage left." Rather than putting up a struggle, you emotionally check out by expressing indifference or apathy. In effect, you're saying, "You can't touch me, because this doesn't matter to me."

Freeze: You become immobilized. Taken aback by the perceived attack, you really do nothing at all.

Remember that no matter which response (or, possibly, responses) you have, they are all learned—a form of auto-pilot. However, you are not meant to go through life on auto-pilot; you need to interrupt these responses before they kick in—to do something different between the time that you encounter a hot button and when you go into your auto-pilot response. Rather than simply plowing ahead with your somewhat misguided auto-pilot at the controls, you need to throw on the brakes and stop the process in its tracks. This "internal stop sign" gives you time to put yourself back in control—to consider choices and options that would never have occurred to you had you allowed the auto-pilot to continue on its course.

As we said, it isn't easy. After all, habit is powerful, almost effortless. Changing those habits demands your energy and attention. But you can do it. Here's a sampling of "internal stop sign" strategies that can help derail your auto-pilot response to difficult situations:

- Count to ten.

- Take a deep, slow breath.

- Consider the other person's perspective and see it in a compassionate, non-judgmental light.

- If there's time, talk a short walk to cool down.

- Take the time to consider any long-range objectives or goals that are important to the situation.

You can try one or more of these or brainstorm some other approaches. Whichever internal stop sign you use, you are interrupting your auto-pilot and injecting choice into the situation.

Experiment with MAGIC

Think about what your gut reaction might be to a customer's complaining—is it fight, flight, or freeze? How do you see that complaint? Do you often view complaints as a form of attack?

Now that you have the concept of an internal stop sign under your belt, think about how you can approach the idea of customer complaint in a different fashion. If you consider the situation, how can you think and react so as not to fall into the fight, flight, or freeze quagmire?

It can be helpful to practice these concepts. Pair off with someone who acts as a customer with a complaint. Employ an internal stop sign; catch yourself and consider ways to approach that person in a constructive, effective manner. The more you practice, the better skilled you'll become in short-circuiting your ineffective auto-pilot responses to hot buttons.

PUTTING CHOICE INTO PRACTICE

Often when a customer has a legitimate complaint, she can become frustrated when she feels that no one is listening or that nothing seems to be happening. This frustration can make her emotional—often to the point that the emotion forces the issue at hand into a secondary role. In these situations, it's all the more critical to employ MAGIC to address both the emotions and the issue that really matters.

In general terms, here's how that process can break down into individual components:

1. The customer calls, and you respond with a welcoming, upbeat greeting.

2. The customer begins to talk and at this point you sense from his words or tone that he is upset, angry, or in some other emotional state. At this point, the importance of listening without interrupting becomes paramount.

3. While listening, you decide how to respond appropriately. It's important to respond with empathy, as we have covered in previous material. However, the words you choose will depend on the emotion and style of the caller:

    a. If the caller is loud, demanding, or irate, or is making accusations and engaging in other forms of strong behavior, it is important to acknowledge his feelings and respond appropriately. Some suggestions:

        "I can see that you're angry, and I do understand your concern."

        "I recognize that this is urgent and am ready to help."

    b. If the caller is anxious, irritated, or distraught, then you may choose a different response, such as

        "I can hear how upset you are. It must have been difficult to call, and I'm here to help."

        "I can sense how unnerving this has been for you. I can help you right now."

4. Use the customer's name as soon as possible. This is essential to establish a personal tie with the customer, reinforcing his confidence that no matter the emotion at hand, you will address his concerns. Using his name also helps focus his attention, freeing it from the dominance of emotion.

5. Make it clear to the caller that you intend to help, then ask permission to obtain whatever additional information may be necessary to begin resolving the issue.

DEFUSING IRATE AND ABUSIVE CALLERS

Unfortunately, sometimes callers go beyond being merely upset or angry. They cross a line into irrational anger or outright abuse. When you encounter these callers, you need to take some very specific steps:

1. **Do not take the abuse personally.** Granted, this can be difficult to do. But it's essential to countering abuse or anger that's simply out of control. Taking that kind of behavior personally only fuels further abuse.

2. **Watch the tone of your voice.** We mentioned earlier how important tone is in all calls; it is particularly so when a caller becomes extremely angry or abusive. At the outset of the call, employ empathic tone and phrases. Doing so can often defuse even the most upset caller.

3. **If the caller continues, use his name and explain what you can do.** Sometimes empathy doesn't cool a particularly angry or abusive caller. If that's the case, use his name and let him know in plain terms what you are willing to do to address the situation.

   "Mr. Jones, I'm here to help you, and I'll do everything I can to resolve this."

   "Sara, I know this has been difficult. I assure you that I can help you."

4. **If the abuse continues, explain that you can't do anything if the caller continues to behave in that manner.**

   "Mr. Phelps, I am ready to help you. I'll be able to do that if you can stop using that sort of language."

   "Ms. Fosse, I'd like to help. If you continue to yell and use profanity, I'll have no choice but to end this call."

5. **Above all, be rational.** Other approaches, such as becoming emotional your-self or acting domineering, may only fuel a caller's emotion. Being calm and rational is the most effective strategy to defuse anger or abuse.

DEALING WITH DISTRAUGHT CALLERS

Sometimes the most difficult callers aren't necessarily abusive. Rather, they're dis-traught, upset, or beside themselves with worry or anxiety. Addressing these callers in the most effective fashion requires some specific strategies:

1. **Use the person's name and express empathy.** That immediate connection can often have a calming effect. Some ideas:

   "Mr. Smith, I can hear this is difficult for you. I'd be happy to take the time to help you right now."

   "This sounds like an awkward situation, Mr. Bosworth. I'd like to ask a few questions to get us headed toward a solution. Would that be all right?"

2. **If the caller is too upset, suggest that she call back.** Occasionally, nothing can really calm someone who's simply too distraught. If that's the situation, sug-gest that she call back later when she feels ready to discuss the issue at hand.

A **MAGIC** Moment

Any of us can become distraught on the phone, given the "right" circum-stances. A colleague of ours trained in MAGIC had that very experience:

"I recently called my health care insurer about my prescription coverage. I had followed all the steps to renew a prescription over their website, but the pre-scription was rejected. I needed it in five days, so I called the suggested number in a panic. Then I started wondering if I'd made a mistake with my coverage—I was beside myself with worry.

"When the customer service rep answered, I was nervous and tense, and ex-pecting the worst. I blurted out my concerns frantically. He calmly asked my name and then used it in the conversation; he assured me that he would help and began to take down the information I shared. It turned out there was a glitch in the system, and my prescription coverage was active. He promised to order the medicine immediately and told me I would receive it in three days.

"When he thanked me for calling at the end, I was relieved, and genuinely thanked him for helping me with this stressful situation. Because of the service he provided, I would never consider changing prescription plans."

REINING IN RAMBLING CALLERS

Rambling callers are often the most frustrating of all. Rather than being upset or abusive, they're simply all over the place—chatting idly, talking about irrelevant topics, and generally taking the conversation anywhere except where it needs to go. Here are some ideas to help rein in such callers:

1. **Politely interrupt.** Use the caller's name if you have it. If not, apologize for the interruption, tell him you'll help, and ask for his name. From there, begin moving the conversation back toward a reasonable progression.

    "Excuse me for interrupting. May I ask some questions so I can help you? May I have your name, please? Mr. Walbridge, I . . ."

2. **Ask how you can help.**

    "Mr. Hurst, I'm sorry to cut in. May I ask how I can help you today?"

3. **Be specific to address the catchpoint.**

    "Jimmy, I'm sorry to break in like this. Am I hearing that you didn't get adequate customer support for that software?"

4. **Let the caller know what you can do.**

    "I apologize for the interruption, Geraldo. I can call shipping and be back in touch with you by 5 PM today. Would that be suitable?"

5. **Summarize, then say what you'll do.**

    "Bill, sorry to interrupt. I just want to be clear that your concern is that the shipment may be going to Portland, Maine, instead of Portland, Oregon. Is that right? Very well, I'll call the shipping manager and get back to you with a definite answer by noon today."

6. **Remember, interrupting is not only suitable but a must.** Interrupting others may be bad manners in most circles, but vital when dealing with a rambling caller.

DELIVERING BAD NEWS

Things don't always happen as planned. People make mistakes, orders go awry, items are back-ordered, and so on. In these kinds of situations, it's you who has the unenviable task of delivering the bad news. That's when you break out the "bad news burger": just sandwich the bad news between two relationship-oriented statements.

Top bun: empathize appropriately given the situation.

Meat: deliver the bad news.

Bottom bun: end on a positive note, such as with additional empathy or help.

Here are some examples:

Top bun: "Mr. Mattes, I understand your concern about your coverage."

Meat: "I carefully reviewed your policy and found that jewelry is not covered in the rider."

Bottom bun: "I know that this is not what you hoped to hear. May I suggest that we update your coverage so that you can avoid this situation in the future?"

Top bun: "Ms. Matlock, I know this has been a great inconvenience for you."

Meat: "I regret that I'm not able to issue your new card today."

Bottom bun: "I appreciate your patience and will send you the card next week."

THE BOTTOM LINE: RESTORING THE RELATIONSHIP

The various sets of steps we outlined in this chapter boil down to one primary objective: restoring a relationship that, at the outset of the call, may have been in jeopardy. If you follow them, you will also accomplish the following:

- You'll gain (or regain) control of the situation.
- You'll shorten and focus your interaction with the caller.
- You'll lower the stress associated with the call.
- You'll boost your own confidence in the service you provide as well as in your ability to handle challenging callers.

All this comes from a focus on the customer and his experience of the situation and from your willingness and ability to help.

MAGIC **Maxims**

- Treat a complaint as an opportunity for improvement, both in service as well as in customer relationships.

- Restore a relationship by listening carefully to an upset caller, expressing empathy, then moving toward a constructive conclusion.

- Don't take abuse personally, but don't tolerate it. Be rational. If a caller persists in being abusive, suggest that the call end.

- Be empathic with distraught callers.

- Don't be afraid to interrupt rambling callers to get the conversation in proper focus.

- Deliver bad news with the "bad news burger": start with empathy and an apology if it's appropriate, deliver the bad news, and end on a positive note.

PART FIVE

The World of MAGIC

A Culture of Exceptional Service

A truly MAGIC culture is a "community of leaders" who embrace a service mind-set and build relationships with employees and customers. It is this type of culture that can deliver exceptional service on a consistent basis—not as a freak occurrence or singular experience, but as the norm.

Let's take a closer look at that definition. First, the term *community of leaders.* The idea behind it is that people throughout the organization genuinely embody the principles of service excellence and, in turn, promote and support those values. There is a shared commitment to Making A Great Impression on the Customer. In that sense, every individual in the organization, at every level, can be a leader, both through that person's own actions and in the message and mind-set he or she conveys to others.

Notice, too, that a service culture refers to the experience of both employees and customers. Research shows that there is a direct correlation between satisfied employees and satisfied customers. Often overlooked or minimized, the employee experience is a vital factor in creating an exceptional customer experience.

Experiment with MAGIC

Here's an opportunity for you to explore whether there is shared understanding of quality service for your organization. Select a recorded call that was a challenge for an agent. Pick one in which the agent displayed both strong and weak elements in the interaction.

Play the tape for your leadership team and ask them to give the call a score of between 1 and 33 points. A score of 33 means it's the best the leadership could hope for. It's perfectly aligned with your organization's vision of quality. A score of 1 means it couldn't have been worse.

Don't let the team members share or look at each other's scores. Simply collect and read the numbers aloud in front of the group. How did you do? Were the scores similar, or not?

In companies that have not invested in service or soft skills, there may be a wide range of numbers. The more variation in numbers, the less the team is aligned around performance expectations. If the disparity is low—if the scores are, say, between three to five points of each other—that could mean that the team is aligned around performance and has a shared understanding of what quality service sounds like. In most cases, this exercise will create lots of discussion, especially if there is a great deal of variation.

A **MAGIC** Moment

Take a look at what MAGIC has done for Community Health Group in Chula Vista, California:

"When MAGIC entered our lives in 1999, those of us who were fortunate to be trained as trainers had little idea of how fast our corporate culture was about to change. It seemed overnight one could overhear coworkers teasing each other with, 'Ouch, that was tragic' or 'You need to add some MAGIC to that letter.'

"The next thing we knew, our human resource department created 'MAGIC Star of the Month' recognizing employees who received thank-you notes from our customers. MAGIC Star employees are highlighted in our monthly staff newsletter and bulletin board, receive recognition at our monthly staff meeting, are entered into a drawing for 'MAGIC Star of the Month Parking Space,' and are given a handwritten congratulatory letter from our CEO.

"All new employees receive the full two-day training, and we provide annual two-hour refresher training on handling difficult customers. We remind our staff of the importance of empathy.

"These trainings help keep our staff focused on delivering exemplary customer service to our 100,000 members. As a nonprofit, locally based health plan dedicated to serving the underserved, our staff uses The 33 Points of MAGIC on a daily basis. Whether it is helping a mom find a pediatrician for her newborn, assisting a physician with a billing question, or educating members on how to properly use the emergency room, effective and empathic communication is essential.

"Our staff takes customer service seriously, and they now have the tools they need to perform at their peak level. They say that The 33 Points give them a newfound confidence to work with our members.

"Our members have noticed a difference too. According to CEO Norma Diaz, 'We have noticed a dramatic improvement in the feedback from our members and physicians.'

"We are 100 percent dedicated to the MAGIC philosophy and to building a culture of unparalleled service and quality care."

PLANNING BEFORE YOU START

Let's say you're interested in building a culture of exceptional service. Before you begin an initiative, consider these key questions and issues:

- Determine the sponsor of the initiative—the person behind the drive to establish a new culture.
- Describe the world you live in. What policies, systems, business objectives, and customers influence you every day?
- Align the initiative with your business strategy and clarify the expected business results.
- Identify the following:
    - Barriers to change in the organization and what can be done about them
    - The level of employee readiness to receive and implement the ideas of the initiative
    - Initial roles and responsibilities for each stage in the initiative
    - How much of the organization you will engage, and at what point
    - A flexible communication plan

BUILDING YOUR SERVICE CULTURE

The next sections describe a process you can use to begin building your service culture.

Assessment

Where you are now can have a powerful influence on the implementation of the initiative. All future expectations need to be anchored in an accurate understanding of current reality, or you're setting yourself up for misunderstanding and possible failure.

We suggest three different types of assessments:

1. **Current service culture.** What's your culture like now? Does it drive or inhibit the delivery of great service? Your norms, values, systems, and processes all influence the culture within which you operate.

2. **Customer perception of service.** What would your customers say about the level of service you provide? It's surprising how many companies just don't know!

3. **Quality of service interactions.** How do your associates measure up? Are you using a comprehensive and objective measure based on behaviors associated with great service? Your standard, or lack of one, will determine the level of service you provide.

Our research over the past twenty-five years suggests that there are five categories of competency that characterize exceptional service cultures. Explore these elements as they relate to your organization. In which areas are you strong? Where are your biggest opportunities? We suggest that you revisit these elements on a regular basis to ensure that you are set up to sustain the service you seek.

1. **Shared service vision and values.** Clear, compelling shared vision and organizational values support and inspire associates to strive for excellence. They emphasize an exceptional experience for employees and customers and are aligned with the strategic direction of the organization.

2. **Service-focused leaders.** Leaders at all levels passionately model the service mind-set, value the contribution of every employee, and focus on constantly improving the customer's total experience.

3. **Consistent service delivery and measurement.** The standards for service delivery are clear, consistent, and integrated. Established measures for face-to-face, phone, and Web interactions are shared by all and practiced with employees and customers.

4. **Developmental training and coaching.** Training is provided to all employees so they can develop the attitude, communication skills, and knowledge to provide an exceptional customer experience. Developmental performance coaching identifies and promotes service contributions and individual growth.

5. **Constant systemic improvement and reinforcement.** Systems and processes throughout the organization are constantly improved and aligned with the service vision and values.

Alignment

As leader of the initiative (or as part of a leadership team), you need to consider how it fits with your business objectives. Do your vision and values align with this initiative? How will standards and measures be defined? How will you align your systems and processes so that they encourage rather than discourage service excellence?

Alignment doesn't deal only with business objectives, vision, values, standards, systems, and processes. People need to be aligned as well. Think about how to engage everyone in the organization—starting with senior executives and moving through to the front line.

- Have you identified which senior executives are crucial to the success of the initiative? If so, how will you engage them to participate? How will you encourage them to model the new behaviors that embody service excellence?

- Have you identified how you will build support for the initiative? How can you engage "natural" leaders throughout the organization so that they communicate, model, and encourage the new mind-set and skills?

Training and Development

Now it's time to develop your people so that they have the skills and attitude that align with your service vision. It's important for everyone to be on the same page. Create a comprehensive plan that addresses the following:

- Who needs training?
- What skills need to be addressed and how?
- How will you tailor the training to specific functions and roles?
- What is the timing?

Be sure the training relates to the specific challenges your associates face every day. There is nothing more effective than recording skill practices and letting your associates hear how they sound. This can be a real eye-opener and just what's needed to change behavior.

You can also give every one of your associates a copy of this book so that they all know what it takes to Make A Great Impression on the Customer!

Reinforcement

You've begun to create the ideal climate for growing service excellence. Now it's time to reinforce skills and attitudes you've introduced. Be sure your reinforcement plan includes the following:

- Reward and recognition systems that clearly reward the right behavior and attitudes
- Leadership communication and modeling ("walking the talk")
- Consistent coaching and feedback
- Review of internal systems and processes that have an impact on the employee and customer experience

Take a look at the following stories to see how other companies reinforce MAGIC service.

The Service Excellence Wall

The impact MAGIC has had on our internal and external interactions here at GBC (a division of ACCO Brands) in the Customer Care division has resulted in the creation of a "$ervice Ex$ellence" Wall.

The wall was created as a way to celebrate the positive comments we receive from our customers. As managers receive compliments from customers on the exceptional service they experienced, a $ervice Ex$ellence citation is placed on the wall. The citation includes a quote from a customer, the associate's name, and a synopsis of that exceptional interaction. Due to the volume of positive comments we receive, we are only able to display three months' worth of these recognitions.

Visitors to our Customer Care floor are immediately drawn to the wall and witness the power of MAGIC.

A MAGIC Store for Exceptional Service

I developed a "MAGIC Store" for our call center representatives. Based on meeting and exceeding their daily standards, going over and above for their external and internal customers, they are able to earn tickets daily that they are able to redeem for various items at the MAGIC Store on a quarterly basis. This creates excitement and enthusiasm as they look for ways to focus on and exceed their customer service standards! We are able to incorporate our company's core values and mission along with the MAGIC model to educate and motivate our call center representatives.

Promotions to Emphasize Each Point

Monthly promotions based on specific MAGIC points have proven effective in keeping a dedicated focus on each behavior.

For example: the Empathy Stick. Based on MAGIC Points 5 and 6, each audited call that effectively demonstrates empathy receives an Empathy Stick (a large candy stick full of powdered candy). They make a big hit, and you can hear the focus on using sincere empathy with words and tone throughout the center!

Once you've done your planning and implemented the four steps we've described here, you can watch the MAGIC momentum build. As the new culture takes hold, it begins to spread and reinforce itself, affecting everything it touches. Employees treat each other better, and they go out of their way to help one another and the customer. You know it's a MAGIC culture when employees willingly help others and go beyond what's expected without being asked, told, or required. Next thing you know, you have an organization where people love their place of work and customers love doing business with you.

MAGIC **Maxims**

- A truly MAGIC culture is a community made up of leaders at all levels who embrace a service mind-set and build relationships with employees and customers.

- Building an exceptional service culture takes more than reading a book or attending a class. It's a four-step process involving assessment, alignment, training and development, and reinforcement.

- When you reinforce and nurture your service culture, you'll have an organization where people love their place of work and customers love doing business with you.

The MAGIC Coach

Think a moment about your favorite individual athlete or sports team. Chances are good that you admire their skill, perhaps their work ethic, or some other aspect of their athleticism that has helped them rise to the top of their sport.

Regardless of the sport—or, for that matter, whether it's a single person or a team made up of dozens of individuals—all successful athletes share one common feature: a coach. That's someone who knows his or her sport well and, through instruction and other hands-on techniques, works with the athlete or team to help bring out their best in every possible situation.

In this regard, MAGIC is like a sport. Once trained, people can become quite skilled—with commitment and practice, that is. But to help them release their full potential and function at an optimal level, a coach is an absolute must. Like an individual athlete or a sports team, every employee can benefit from the guidance, feedback, and inspiration of a coach.

Research has shown the powerful impact of coaching in business settings. For example, *HR Magazine* (Mar. 1996) reported that 90 percent of American workers who received on-the-job coaching or mentoring believed it was an effective development tool. Unfortunately, only 33 percent of the workforce has ever had a coach or mentor.

Simply put: coaching matters. And being a good coach matters even more. If you're reading this, you're probably interested in being a coach yourself (or know someone who is). That's great. Let's get started!

WHO CAN BE A MAGIC COACH?

Almost anyone can become a coach. Where he or she happens to be in a company or organization is a secondary consideration. Far more important is the person's attitude and his or her belief that MAGIC can truly empower others and create a positive experience for them. Simply put, the most effective coach guides and mentors others in a way that releases their potential, and in so doing contributes to the goals and objectives of the organization.

Coaching skills can thus benefit anyone who has the willingness and desire to help others learn and grow.

WHAT MAKES A GREAT COACH?

Take a moment to think back in your own life to someone—a coach, perhaps, or some other leader—who had a great influence on you. What made that person a great coach? Why do you recall the experience as vividly as you do?

Now think of what that coach actually did. How did she motivate or encourage you? Did she perhaps get you to believe in yourself when your inclination was to do otherwise? How did she support you and help you move beyond where you were?

Most people say that the coach who most motivated and inspired them saw them not only as they were but also as they *might be*. In other words, the coach saw beyond their current performance to what they could do and become. The coach truly saw their potential.

As a coach, you are of course "instructing" the people you're coaching—but you have the unique opportunity to do much more than that. You're serving as a living model of the principles of MAGIC, a model that emphasizes a belief in others and their potential. That's as powerful a form of coaching as you could ever hope to offer.

A **MAGIC** Moment

A manager in an insurance company shared the impact these coaching principles had on his perspective and performance:

"I have a team of twelve people reporting to me, yet two associates always seemed to be an issue for me. They were consistently poor performers; every month their numbers would be significantly lower than everyone else's. Yet I knew that they had received the same directions, went to team meetings, and got the same reports and documents as everyone else. It seemed that they just couldn't perform to our standards. I always considered them to be 'real problems,' and I lamented the fact that they were on my team. Lucky me. I was stuck with them.

"I now have a whole new perspective on my role as coach. I thought of those poor performers and asked myself, 'What part of their performance do I own?' I realized that, as their coach, I owned the results of *all* of my associates, even the underperformers. Once I realized this, I knew that I had to change the way I communicated with these individuals. I needed to find a way to coach them that worked for them. So I took the time to listen to them and really coach them, helping them achieve the goals they set for themselves. The turnabout was amazing. Their performance improved dramatically, and now other team members turn to them for help.

"And, most important, I look at my role and myself a lot differently now. I know that I am responsible for my team's output and the way I communicate with them and others. I feel different, and I know my team feels the difference too."

WHAT DOES A COACH DO?

A coach is someone who is committed to

- Developing and maintaining effective coaching relationships with associates
- Guiding and supporting the development of associates
- Holding associates accountable for performance goals and contributions to the team

In other words, the coach models two core principles: respect for the person and accountability for results. The coach understands that he plays an integral role in the experience that associates have as members of the organization.

It's probably clear by now that MAGIC coaching sets a standard. The common phrase "walk the talk" that is so popular in leadership circles has a particular meaning here. Because MAGIC is about attitude expressed through behavior, anyone familiar with its principles will be readily able to judge when a coach is walking the talk. In organizations across the country, participants in our programs ask us, "Will my boss be taking this class?" and "Is this class for *everyone* in our company?" These are heartfelt questions. The associates who ask them want to know two things:

- Will I be treated with more respect as a result of MAGIC?

- Is my boss also accountable for being MAGIC?

Any response short of "yes" calls the organization's commitment into question. So how does a coach "step up to the plate"? We suggest the following:

- Develop and increase your own capacity for MAGIC—be a model of these skills and attitudes for others.

- Develop your ability to lead and encourage others as they also develop their skills and attitudes.

- Develop your ability to *lead yourself* by focusing on what you control and what you can influence in a positive way.

A **MAGIC** Moment

A facilitator shared this poignant story from a program on coaching:

"On the first day of the program, I asked the participants to pair up for a skill practice. Mindy, a manager in the program, was sitting next to Carol, a supervisor who reported to her. Mindy and Carol clearly had a good relationship; it was obvious that they liked and respected one another. And even though I encouraged them to pair up with others for their skill practice, they insisted on doing theirs together. When it came time to debrief what happened, Mindy made a contribution to the class that I will never forget.

"She said that as a woman with a disability, she always felt that she had to work a little harder to demonstrate that she was a capable, knowledgeable professional. She went on to say that one of the ways she did this was to make sure she had all the answers when her employees found themselves in a tough spot. She said, 'I now realize that the best way to demonstrate my ability is to encourage and acknowledge the ability of others. By doing all the talking and all the problem solving, I was actually shutting down Carol's good thinking!' Everyone looked at Carol. Carol smiled, nodded in agreement, and said, 'I feel like now we can really put our heads together and get even more done!'"

ESTABLISHING THE COACHING RELATIONSHIP

So let's assume that your commitment to personal development and modeling is solid. How then do you, the coach, go about coaching? You begin by recognizing that coaching is as much a process as it is a skill. That means starting with the relationship first, much as you do when you "make a connection with a customer" before you proceed to the situation or task.

This makes sense. No one—particularly someone who has not received any sort of coaching in the past—is likely to be overly responsive to a supervisor or even a colleague who suddenly announces that he's her coach. Rather, treating an associate with respect begins with letting her know why you're there and what's going to happen in this coaching relationship.

The overall process for establishing your coaching relationship consists of four steps:

1. **Purpose.** The first thing you want to do as a coach is to explain "the big picture," to answer two burning yet often unvoiced questions: "What is this about?" and "Why?" Let's say you are meeting with each associate individually. Here's how you might begin:

   > "Trevor, as you heard at the quarterly meeting last week, the company is really focusing on the experience our customers have with us. I'd like to follow up on that very topic along the lines of the MAGIC training you received. And I'd like to explore how I might coach you going forward."

   Comments to this effect let you share where you would like to go with your coaching and how it fits in with the organization's goals.

2. **Perceptions.** Once you've established the purpose of your coaching, actively engage your associate in a two-way conversation. Here you invite the associate with a question, such as "What are your thoughts about that?" You then listen empathically.

3. **Possibilities.** When you have a good sense of what your associate is thinking and feeling about coaching, ask her if she has any specific objective or goal she'd like to tackle first. For example, what aspect of her communication skills would she like to improve or change? You might ask if any of The 33 Points of MAGIC are confusing; they too can be first goals. In exploring possibilities, also ask how you can help her work toward whatever goal she identifies, and what she can do to improve. Only after exploring your ideas and those of your associate do you move to the next step.

4. **Pact.** Finally, it's important that both you and your associate agree on what's going to happen next and who will do what by when. You might summarize the pact by saying, "We each agree to assess twelve customer interactions against The 33 Points of MAGIC within the next two weeks. We'll compare our perceptions of these calls at our next coaching session." Other types of agreements related to developing these skills might include the following:

- Peer coaching: a colleague listens to a peer's customer conversations and offers feedback.

- Self-assessment: an employee listens to recordings of himself and assesses his own performance.

- Additional role playing with others to practice skills.

Experiment with MAGIC

When we work with organizations specifically to develop a coaching program, we emphasize the importance of role playing to enhance learning by doing. Through role playing, a prospective coach gains a feel for how she nurtures relationships with others and helps them release their potential. Such skill practice creates a baseline from which to continue to develop as a coach.

Follow our lead. With a colleague, role-play a coaching conversation in which you are working to establish a coaching relationship. Go through the four steps we just described. Switch roles. Share feedback on what you thought was effective and what was confusing or even unsettling. If you want to, tape your practice. This can be particularly useful in your development as a coach.

PREPARING FOR THE NEXT COACHING SESSION

Having established the coaching relationship, you now follow through on your end of the "pact," the agreements you made with your associate. As we mentioned, these can take any number of forms. Perhaps you listen directly to conversations with customers as they're occurring. Maybe you listen to tapes or audio files. In any case, if you're assessing someone else, it's helpful to have The 33 Points of MAGIC for reference as you listen. That can help you identify those points your associate is demonstrating, as well as those that may need further work.

This is important for several reasons. First, you want to be as specific as you can so as to provide accurate feedback that can be discussed and then acted on. Second, you want to identify your associate's strengths as well as those skills that need development.

Having fulfilled the agreements from the first coaching session, it's time to prepare for the second. The components of this meeting mirror those of the first session:

- A review of your agreement with the person you're coaching—the goal he wanted to achieve and the way the two of you agreed to address it

- The employee's assessment of his performance toward that goal

- Your assessment, supported by feedback based on observable behaviors

- Joint exploration of how to proceed, including recommendations, alternative strategies, and other approaches to development

- Agreement on action steps for both you and the person you're coaching

Several MAGIC communication skills have particular impact in a coaching session. These include rephrasing and empathizing.

To illustrate, if an employee says she becomes jumpy when a caller expresses irritation, rephrase what she said to confirm you heard her correctly: "Are you saying that you tend to become anxious when a caller gets angry or annoyed?" Empathy builds the relationship by reinforcing that as a coach, you understand those reactions and are committed to helping: "I understand that it can be hard to keep cool when a customer reacts that way."

The following are some other effective behaviors:

- **Ask her what's working.** "I noticed that you used the customer's name at an appropriate spot. Did you get a sense that it helped make a connection?"

- **Acknowledge improvement.** If your associate fails to notice a point that you consider an improvement, be sure to point it out to him.

- **Suggest improvement when needed.** "At this point in the conversation, I noticed that your empathy dropped off some. Do you hear that? What do you think you could have done differently?"

- **Have her suggest the next goal.** "What have you decided to work on next? How do you think you'd like to approach that?"

- **Agree on next steps.** "It sounds like expressing greater empathy is the next goal you'd like to tackle. Let's agree on what you and I will both do before our next meeting."

The focus of follow-up meetings is to keep moving forward in a comfortable, systematic progression—moving toward your associate's goals while building a strong relationship between you and the person you're coaching.

Experiment with MAGIC

If you can, practice follow-up coaching sessions with others. Have them critique you on

- How you come across
- How specific you are in your feedback and recommendations
- How supportive an environment you establish for future progress

Again, this sort of practice can prove helpful in making sure you come across as a caring, supportive, and committed coach.

TWO-MINUTE COACHING

No matter how committed you might be to coaching, it's not always possible to earmark enough time to have the planned and scheduled coaching sessions we just outlined. (Those may take ten to twenty minutes or even longer, depending on what you're covering and with whom you're working.) That makes two-minute coaching sessions particularly valuable.

If you already have an established coaching relationship, two-minute coaching sessions can happen on the fly. You may be walking by someone's desk when you hear something you'd like to follow up on from a coaching perspective. For instance, the employee blurts out: "If I hear another customer complain about the wait time, I'm going to scream!"

Here, start by recalling what you and this associate have addressed in any prior coaching sessions. Chances are good that doing so will give you a basis for connecting your current observation with a topic or area of growth the two of you have already discussed. Next, remember the importance of rephrasing and empathy.

You might start by saying, "Trish, it sounds like you've had some tough calls today." *(Let her explain.)*

Then you might say, "Wow—you've had a difficult morning. I know that you wanted to work on choosing more effective responses in situations like this."

After discussing possible responses, ask, "What can you do to get back on track?"

Connecting with your associate in this way can be just what she needs to feel supported and guided in the heat of the moment. You've let her do most of the talking, and, through your rephrasing and empathy, she is likely to come up with a suitable next step on her own.

Don't expect these brief coaching opportunities to solve every problem (although they may solve more than you expect). What they can do is establish a suitable agenda for more substantive coaching sessions later on—and, in the process, further build your relationship with others as a coach.

COACHING AS AN ONGOING PROCESS

It's clear by now that coaching MAGIC is far from a one-shot deal. Rather, it's an ongoing series of conversations and actions, one that requires commitment and effort. The process looks something like this:

1. Establish the coaching relationship.
2. Observe.
3. Coach.
4. Reinforce.
5. Coach (and refocus as needed).
6. Observe.

You've learned some of the practical skills that contribute to effective coaching. But underlying what it takes to be a great coach is your attitude and mind-set. Let's have a look at those.

ADOPTING AN INTERNAL LOCUS OF CONTROL

Few sports teams or athletes would excel if their coaches treated their coaching responsibility with indifference—as though there were much more valuable ways they'd like to spend their time.

Even the best-prepared, most highly motivated MAGIC coach on the planet can do little good if she cannot find the time to develop her team. Perhaps the underlying challenge is that the organization is not particularly supportive of her effort to coach, preferring that she focus on meetings or reports. These kinds of factors can have a negative impact on a sincere effort to be an effective coach.

Sound familiar? Let's take a look at the various forces that may affect your ability to coach—and what you can and can't do about them.

Start with a review of your organization. What supports your ability to become an effective coach, and what stands in the way?

Experiment with MAGIC

The two different forces we just referred to are known as driving and restraining forces. One encourages and enables you to do what you wish to do, and the other does pretty much the opposite.

Take a sheet of paper and divide it into two vertical columns. On the left-hand side, list all the driving forces in your organization—those that support your coaching. Next, fill out the other side with every restraining force you can think of—those that hinder you.

Now consider the two lists as a whole. What forces do you spend more time thinking about? Are the restraining forces an ongoing source of discouragement and frustration? How do you work to be effective in the face of these influences?

Early in this chapter we suggested that a coach's development includes leading himself by focusing on what he can control and what he can influence in a positive way. In other words, we have returned to the idea of locus of control, which we have discussed elsewhere in this book.

Let's take our discussion of locus of control a step further. Research has shown that people tend to adopt one of two forms of locus of control—external and internal. If you have an external locus of control, you hold the attitude that your life is dictated by forces outside your control and that you pretty much have to take what you're given.

If you adopt an internal locus of control, you put more into your own hands. Your attitude hinges on a belief that to a large extent you make your own luck—that through your hard work and perseverance, you can largely control what happens to you.

Just where you fall on the scale between internal and external will greatly influence how effective you are as a coach. For example, a coach with an external locus of control who feels pressured by a lack of time for coaching might simply give up, losing valuable opportunities to do two-minute coaching. Such a coach sees challenges and setbacks as things over which she has little or no influence. She also tends to react in an emotional fashion, which is generally unproductive.

An internal focus, in contrast, is far more constructive. A coach with an internal locus of control believes she can influence things for the better, and thus leads herself more effectively. She can respond with greater awareness and responsibility. With this focus, she seizes every small opportunity to coach, even if it is a series of two-minute coaching conversations.

Think about your locus of control as you coach. Yes, restraining forces are real. But by working to adopt a more internal locus of control—by identifying those elements both inside you and outside that you can genuinely influence—you're focusing on what you *can* do. You're taking a proactive stance that will help you manage the restraining forces in your organization.

THE LIST OF TEN

Coaches pay particular attention to valuing people in demonstrable ways. Think of this as taking such MAGIC phrases as "Thank you" and "I appreciate" further. You do so by acknowledging people for their effort, contributions, triumphs, and sometimes simply their hard-won progress.

Naturally, most organizations have a variety of formal ways of acknowledging success, such as positive performance evaluations, promotions, and other rewards.

But the smaller things you can do to acknowledge the people you coach are limitless. And they often matter just as much, because your actions can be more specific and personal, reinforcing the relationship you have established.

Here is our "List of Ten"—ideas we have culled from great MAGIC coaches across the country that let their teams know how much they are appreciated. Use these as is, or modify them to suit your personal style:

1. Make congratulating someone an event. Call your associate into your office, mention the achievement, and express a heartfelt and substantive thank-you. Or have a team "standing ovation" to really surprise and delight an associate.

2. Post a gallery of photographs that show employees who have distinguished themselves in some fashion—a "wall of fame," if you like.

3. Start meetings by pointing out someone's specific achievement. This can be a great motivator for everyone.

4. Ask senior executives to take time to thank individual employees.

5. Reward solid achievement with time off.

6. Create an award—perhaps a plaque or trophy—to mark a significant individual accomplishment.

7. Create an award for team accomplishments.

8. Arrange special events—lunches or dinners—to mark achievements.

9. Reward solid performance with special assignments or tasks.

10. Mention when you learn something yourself from an associate you have coached.

SELF-ASSESSMENT

One final aspect of the coaching experience is more self-directed and functions as a powerful example of modeling. You evaluate how you are doing as a coach and identify what you can do better.

Take some time every so often to consider questions such as these:

1. What are my coaching strengths?

2. Where can I improve?

3. What can I do to improve?

4. How will I know when I've improved?

As we mentioned earlier, MAGIC coaching is very much an ongoing process—for you as well as for the people you coach. Approach your own progress as enthusiastically as you do that of others, and the results—in performance, work environment, and the way people feel about themselves and others—will undoubtedly show.

MAGIC **Maxims**

- It's important to coach MAGIC to help others improve skills they have learned.
- Start working with employees by first establishing a coaching relationship.
- Use a four-step coaching process in which you focus on (1) the purpose of the session, (2) your associate's perceptions and your own, (3) possibilities to explore, and (4) the pact of agreements and actions to follow.
- Coach regularly—both in scheduled meetings and in brief two-minute sessions.
- Think about others who have inspired you and brought out your best. Remember that the best coaches focus on both performance and potential.
- Approach coaching as an ongoing process—both for the people you coach and in terms of your performance as a coach.

MAGIC Face-to-Face

L et's face it—it's much tougher to stand three feet away from an angry customer than it is to talk to one who is a thousand miles away on the telephone. That's why we'll take an up-close and personal look at face-to-face interactions.

A BRIEF REFRESHER

The study we mentioned earlier by Albert Mehrabian showed that if words, tone, or body language conflict, people will believe what they see—not what they hear.

So far we have focused on telephone conversations, where the emphasis is on two elements: tone and words.

Now it's time for the visual to take center stage. That means we need to take a fresh look at those elements that go into making a great impression face-to-face.

A **Tragic** Moment

A friend recounts this story of a discouraging interaction with a guest services associate whose body language spoke volumes:

"I had been traveling all day and finally arrived at a well-known hotel chain. I immediately noticed that the guest services associate at the front desk was busily entering information into the computer. As I stood there waiting for her to acknowledge me, I noticed a statement of promise about how each guest would be treated. Yet it took at least two minutes before the associate looked up to acknowledge me. When she did, she looked annoyed and said in a robotic monotone, 'Are you checking in?'

"She went through the motions of 'checking me in,' but made no effort to connect with me. In fact, there was no enthusiasm at all during our brief interaction. I made eye contact with her and smiled, but she would have none of it. We were about two feet away from each other, separated only by a finely polished counter. But we might as well have been miles apart—because that's how it felt."

Experiment with MAGIC

If you need any further proof of the importance of the visual aspect of face-to-face communication, try this brief exercise. The next time you're having a conversation with someone else, excuse yourself and walk out of his sight for a moment—just far enough so that he can't see what you're doing. Then, adjust something about your appearance—for instance, if you're wearing a tie, stick the end in your shirt pocket. If you're wearing a necklace, try slipping it over your ear. Just do something that alters your appearance in a distinct, perhaps comical fashion.

Now return to your conversation. See how long it takes for the other person to notice the change—and, as likely as not, to ask what you're doing!

This little exercise illustrates how evident the visual can be. Whether you intend to or not, you quickly notice something that's visual—often before the other person has spoken a word. Even more important, your perception of visual information forms an instantaneous impression of that person. In our exercise, the visual element may have been funny, but what if it had been something a bit less amusing—say, a bad stain on your clothes or a zipper that was undone?

Consider a person whose visual impression is unsettling. Couple that with, say, a monotone and a rash of tragic phrases, and you have a communications disaster on your hands.

WHAT MAKES A VISUAL IMPRESSION?

Let's take a look at the visual elements in a face-to-face setting. Please keep in mind that our observations relate mostly to the American experience. Each culture has its own protocols in relation to these key elements.

1. **Facial expression.** Your face says a lot. People will react differently when you smile warmly as opposed to when you look distracted, annoyed, or indifferent. Is your expression warm and inviting or cold and stern? People will make decisions about you just by looking at your facial expression.

2. **Eye contact.** How would you feel if someone kept her eyes on yours *all the time?* What if someone constantly diverts his eyes, making little or no contact? Wouldn't both scenarios make you feel uncomfortable? Would you wonder about the other's motives? Appropriate eye contact flows with the conversation. It sends a message of connection and shows that you're listening; much like the use of the name over the telephone, eye contact makes an essential connection with a customer.

3. **Gestures and movements.** Some gestures and movements naturally convey openness and a desire to make contact. For instance, a firm handshake indicates confidence and a desire for contact with the other person. A flabby or weak handshake, in contrast, can send a message that the person is ill at ease, uninterested, or gun-shy about making contact with someone else.

   Some of us may also have an unconscious habit that is distracting to others. If you twist your hair around your finger, tap your pen against the desk, or jiggle the change in your pocket, people may pay more attention to those distractions than to what you are saying.

4. **Posture.** The Hunchback of Notre Dame may have been misunderstood, but his posture certainly didn't help him any. That's an exaggerated example, but posture does tell a great deal about someone. For instance, a slumped posture may suggest a person who's weary or bored. By the same token, an upright, open posture exudes self-esteem and readiness to help.

5. **Proximity.** There was a television show episode a few years back that featured a "close talker"—an otherwise well-meaning fellow who inadvertently intimidated others by placing his face inches from theirs while he spoke. The space that you establish between yourself and others is an important component of your overall visual impression. Too close, and you're literally "in

someone's face." Too far, and you can come across to others as distant and aloof.

6. **Appearance.** Your overall appearance—your clothes, your grooming, and just the way you carry yourself—says a great deal about you. They may seem trivial, but seemingly "small" things like a wrinkled shirt or worn-out shoes contribute to the impression you make—and what people may think of you whether you realize it or not.

   In addition to good grooming and a professional appearance, consider how to ensure that your overall presentation is appropriate to your role. For example, if you're delivering food to a customer's house, your clothes should be neat and your hands scrupulously clean. Your appearance will definitely affect the customer's perception of the food's quality and freshness.

MAKE A GREAT IMPRESSION AT THE START

If you think about how all these elements work together, it's easy to see just how dominant the visual aspect can be in face-to-face interaction. In these encounters, the visual plays a particularly important role in making another person feel comfortable and confident—before even one word is shared. Just one visual element that's off the mark can be sufficient to derail a conversation from the very beginning.

Let's look at the first few seconds of your face-to-face interaction: your greeting.

1. **Your words.** Welcoming words are an important element of any face-to-face encounter. They should be direct and to the point. If someone approaches you, you might say,

   "Good morning. My name is Cassandra. How may I help you today?"

   If you are approaching someone else, your welcoming words might be

   "Good afternoon. I'm Jeff from R&C Appliances. I'm here to fix your dishwasher."

2. **Upbeat tone.** Your tone should be positive and welcoming—expressing an enthusiasm and genuine interest in serving the customer. Sound like you care and truly want to help!

3. **Pace.** A solid greeting and uplifting tone can be completely undercut by the pace of your speech. Talk too fast, and your words may become jumbled. Too slow, and you'll sound as though you're sleepwalking. Keep the pace

moderate—not too slow, but not so fast that it sounds as though you're pressed for time or too busy to help.

4. **Body language.** This is very much the heart of face-to-face encounters. How you look and the impression you convey say much more than anything that's actually spoken. Some general tips:

   - Have a pleasant facial expression. Smile!
   - Watch your posture. Be upright and open.
   - Make eye contact.
   - Offer a firm handshake when appropriate. Make contact with the thumb joint—two to three pumps at the most.

PUTTING IT ALL TOGETHER

Such elements as empathy, personalization, specificity, establishing deadlines, and confirming agreement are as important in the flesh as they are over the telephone. In face-to-face interactions, however, they operate in concert with the visual aspects we have discussed. Exhibit 19.1 lists The 33 Points of MAGIC for face-to-face interactions.

Exhibit 19.1: The 33 Points of MAGIC—Face-to-Face Interactions

Make a Connection: Build the Relationship

1. Greeting: Offer welcoming words, positive body language (make eye contact, smile, and so on).
2. Greeting: Maintain an upbeat tone.
3. Greeting: Use an unhurried pace.
4. Listen and don't interrupt.
5. Express empathy through words.
6. Express empathy through tone.
7. Use the customer's name as soon as you hear it.
8. Tell him or her that you will help.
9. Ask permission to gain more information.

Exhibit 19.1: The 33 Points of MAGIC—Face-to-Face Interactions, Cont'd.

Act Professionally: Express Confidence

10. Express sincerity and helpfulness through tone.
11. Maintain appropriate pace.
12. Speak clearly with proper volume.
13. Use "I," not "we," when appropriate.
14. Use "please" and "thank you" to show courtesy.
15. Avoid tragic phrases, jargon, and negative body language.
16. Use MAGIC phrases and body language to build confidence and trust.

Get to the Heart of the Matter: Listen and Ask Questions

17. Ask questions to find the catchpoint (the "what" and the "why").
18. Listen and rephrase appropriately.
19. Repeat numbers (four or more) and new contact information.
20. Before interruption, explain why and get permission.
21. After interruption, use the customer's name and thank him or her or apologize.
22. Keep interaction to an appropriate length.

Inform and Clarify What You Will Do

23. Be proactive: Offer options or solutions.
24. Set a deadline or time frame before the customer asks.
25. Educate with relevant information.
26. Be knowledgeable and accurate.
27. Summarize the next step(s).
28. Get agreement on the next step(s).

Close with the Relationship in Mind

29. Offer additional assistance when appropriate.
30. Use the customer's name.
31. End with a MAGIC phrase.
32. Close with a sincere tone and positive body language.
33. Did you lead the interaction closer to resolution?

It's helpful to assess how you handle face-to-face situations. The following are some benchmark questions to consider:

- Did you work with the customer, rather than against him?
- Did you control the interaction in a professional manner?
- Did you remain calm, particularly if the topic of the conversation was emotional or upsetting to the other person?
- Is the person closer to a solution as a result of your interaction?
- Does the other person have a positive impression of you and your organization?

If you can answer yes to these questions, you've done a solid job of applying the principles of MAGIC in a face-to-face setting. Given the complexities of these interactions, that's not always easy to do.

A **MAGIC** Moment

One of our facilitators shared his experience at a restaurant, which went from tragic to MAGIC:

"Recently, I had horrible service at a restaurant in Connecticut. It took forever to get drinks, the server never brought the bread, and dinner took almost forty minutes to deliver. On top of that, the server had a real attitude; it seemed that she couldn't care less about our requests or complaints.

"It was just so bad that I had to complain. When I did, the manager was appalled by what she heard. She came right over to our table and turned the situation around. Here is what she did:

- She introduced herself in a professional way: 'I am Jill the manager here, and my job is to make sure you are totally satisfied with our restaurant.'
- She asked for our names, and even included the child in our party, who is twelve. Not only did she ask for the child's name; she asked her questions on how her experience was.
- Her face and words showed she cared. She expressed empathy when she said, 'I am so sorry you had poor service. Going out to dinner with your family should be a great experience, and I'm sorry that happened to you.'

- She smiled, looked confident, and stated, 'I would be glad to help you myself—what can I do for you to have a better experience?' In fact, she waited on us herself for the remainder of the meal.

- She would not let us pay for the dinner. I told her that that was not my intention when I complained. She replied, 'I could tell that. It was obvious you just wanted a good meal and a better experience.'

"She got my catchpoint and totally changed my impression of the place. It was one of the BEST service experiences I have ever had!"

MAGIC **Maxims**

- In face-to-face encounters, visual impression is the predominant factor in communication—not words or tone.

- A visual impression comprises a variety of elements, including facial expression, posture, gesture and mannerisms, proximity, and eye contact.

- It's important to remember that *you* are the message in a face-to-face contact. People make decisions about you from your body language and visual appearance.

chapter TWENTY

The MAGIC of Relationship Selling

"**N**othing sells like great service, and nothing serves like a great salesperson." This phrase captures the value of both selling and serving—and our suggested approach to sales.

Consider this quotation from an article in the *Journal of Personal Selling and Sales Management* (Liu, A. H., and Leach, M. P. "Developing Loyal Customers with a Value-Adding Sales Force: Examining Customer Satisfaction and the Perceived Credibility of Consultative Salespeople." Spring 2001, p. 147) regarding consultative selling: "Salespeople must be able to communicate knowledge in ways that provide value to customers. They must communicate effectively with both internal customers and external customers, and they must be committed to a long-term relationship where their own profits grow as their customers' do."

Here you'll discover that a service focus and relationship-oriented skills are critical to the sales process—whether you're working with a customer of long standing or about to make a dreaded cold call.

Experiment with MAGIC

There is an array of preconceived notions and stereotypes that are attributed to salespeople. Sometimes they are positive; as often as not, they're not particularly flattering.

Take a few minutes to identify those characteristics and behaviors that you might associate with a salesperson. This exercise may be particularly interesting—perhaps even challenging—if you yourself are a salesperson. Capture your own ideas as well as what you think others might say.

Be as thorough as you can, hitting on both the positive as well as the negative. As an added element, solicit others' participation in this exercise, then combine your lists to see what you've come up with.

Now review your list. There are bound to be some upbeat attributes in the mix—such words as "energetic" and "proactive."

However, you may have listed other words that are less appealing. Did terms like "pushy" and "stubborn" show up on your list? They often do. The fact is, salespeople often get a bum rap.

Whether they're justified or not, those negative attitudes and impressions exist, and we're going to help you counteract them, leaving others with a very different view of what a salesperson can be.

FOCUSING ON THE CUSTOMER

Glance back at some of the words that appeared on your list of descriptive terms. Chances are good that some of them focus on the salesperson himself or herself—words that suggest determination, discipline, and a capacity to overcome disappointment.

But there might not be any words that describe the salesperson's focus on the customer.

That's the heart of the MAGIC approach to sales. Our philosophy emphasizes the importance of placing the customer at the very center of every interaction.

The idea is not to push a product or service on a customer who may be completely uninterested. Nor do we advocate a transactional approach based on slick strategies to get customers to say yes. Rather, we focus on adding value and building a long-term relationship that will benefit both parties.

Here are the core principles:

• Seek to understand a customer's needs and priorities.

- Develop a relationship rather than just make a sale.

- Use initiative and creativity to meet and, if possible, exceed customer expectations.

- Identify challenges that a customer may confront and, in turn, position products and services as solutions to those issues.

- Think ahead to identify long-term customer needs.

- Respond to customers in a consistently professional, expedient, and accurate fashion.

- Act with integrity throughout the relationship.

A **MAGIC** Moment

Here's a story that shows some of these principles in action:

"Eight months pregnant and with a five-year-old, my husband and I bowed to the inevitable and decided to buy a minivan.

"We researched our options and decided on the van we wanted. At the dealership, a friendly salesperson directed us to a van that met all of our specs with one exception: it had captain's chairs in the back seat rather than a bench.

"Captain's chairs were an additional $750 option, and we didn't want them. 'Why do people spend extra for these?' I asked. 'Well, they look nice and they're comfortable,' the salesperson said. 'How about I knock another $300 off the price?' We hemmed and hawed, but ultimately decided to check with another dealership.

"Later that week, I explained the tale to my girlfriend Lisa. Lisa had four-year-old twins and a two-year-old son. 'Captain's chairs! You need them. Don't you remember the arguments you used to have with your brother and sister when they got on 'your side' of the car? You'll have two kids soon. Captain's chairs take care of those annoying arguments. And when you need to grab something from the back seat, you don't have to climb over a bench to get it. Those seats are worth every penny.'

"What she said made perfect sense. We went back to the dealer and bought the car from another salesperson. When we told him which van we wanted, he said, 'Oh, this van is perfect for you with a baby coming—and you will love the fact that these captain's chairs avoid those sibling arguments!'

"This salesperson and my friend Lisa did what the first salesperson neglected to do: paid attention to our family's situation and customized benefit statements to meet our needs. Good-looking backseat chairs meant nothing to us; avoiding arguments and having convenient access to stored materials did. Some observation, questioning, and an understanding of the benefits that applied to us were what made the sale."

When a salesperson focuses on a customer's needs and understands her priorities, he can find a product and benefits that meet them, and win the sale as well as the customer's confidence.

PUTTING IT ALL TOGETHER

How do you put these principles into practice? Although selling occurs both over the phone and face-to-face, let's take a closer look at the approach for an incoming sales call. Exhibit 20.1 lists The 33 Points of MAGIC for relationship selling with incoming calls.

Exhibit 20.1: The 33 Points of MAGIC for Relationship Selling—Incoming Calls

Make a Connection: Build the Relationship and Engage Interest

1. Greeting: Offer welcoming words.
2. Greeting: Maintain an upbeat tone.
3. Greeting: Use an unhurried pace.
4. Listen carefully for needs and concerns—don't interrupt.
5. Express empathy or enthusiasm through words.
6. Express empathy or enthusiasm through tone.
7. Use the customer's name as soon as you hear it.
8. Thank the customer for his or her interest.

Exhibit 20.1: The 33 Points of MAGIC
for Relationship Selling—Incoming Calls, Cont'd.

Act Professionally: Express Confidence

9. Tell the customer how you will help.
10. Ask permission to gain more information, if appropriate.
11. Maintain an appropriate pace.
12. Express sincerity and helpfulness through tone.
13. Speak clearly with proper volume.
14. Use "I," not "we," when appropriate.
15. Avoid tragic phrases and jargon.
16. Use MAGIC phrases to build confidence and trust.

Get to the Heart of the Matter: Determine Customer Needs

17. Refer to customer interests when asking questions.
18. Listen and rephrase appropriately.
19. Ask questions to pinpoint initial needs.
20. Explore needs with focused questions.
21. Repeat numbers (four or more).

Inform and Clarify: Highlight What Your Product Can Do

22. Frame information based on the customer's needs and interests.
23. Communicate benefits—be knowledgeable and accurate.
24. Clarify objections first.
25. Respond to objections with value and benefits to the customer.
26. Summarize options and next steps.

Close with Agreement: End on a Professional Note

27. Get agreement on the next steps toward a sale.
28. Provide reassurance for the customer's action or decision.
29. Use the customer's name.
30. End with a MAGIC phrase.
31. Close with a sincere tone.
32. Are you closer to a sale, or have you closed one?
33. Make follow-up plans and notes.

DID YOU SAY "OBJECTION"?

Consider this scenario based on a real situation experienced by a travel agent in a telephone conversation with a prospect:

Rep: One of our best deals right now would be a lovely one-week stay on the coast of Brazil. It's high 80s, sunny all day, and—

Caller *(interrupting)*: Brazil! I'd never go there!

Rep: I think you'd love it. The weather is just beautiful this time of—

Caller *(interrupting again)*: I said I'd never go there! *(click)*

It's apparent that the representative missed the mark with this prospect. What happened here? Clearly the caller was objecting to the rep's suggestion.

Objections are a fact of life in sales. Our approach to selling begins by "rethinking" objections, by seeing them as requests for more information and, in essence, as opportunities to continue the conversation. Imagine if our scenario had occurred like this:

Rep: One of our best deals right now would be a lovely one-week stay on the coast of Brazil. It's high 80s, sunny all day, and—

Caller: Brazil! I'd never go there!

Rep: Mr. Peters, that's good for me to know. Can you tell me why you feel that way?

Caller: Sure! I heard that place is just for young people—we're not interested in the night life, you know.

Rep: I can see why you'd be concerned. And Mr. Peters, let me assure you that our weekday packages are designed for leisure, shopping, and day trips. We are finding that our more mature customers are interested in excursions like these. May I tell you more?

Caller: I had no idea you had packages for folks like us. Tell me about those day trips—we do like historical sites.

Oh, what a difference clarifying an objection can make. In this scenario, the caller did in fact book the trip to Brazil, but only after the representative used the following approach:

- Clarify the objection. ("Can you tell me why you feel that way?")

- Acknowledge the objection. ("I can see why you'd be concerned.")

- Clarify, prove, or redirect the objection. ("Let me assure you that our weekday packages are designed for leisure, shopping, and day trips.")

  - Clarify: provide more details

  - Prove: give accurate supporting information

  - Redirect: focus on another feature or benefit

This approach works because it is customer focused. Instead of arguing, defending, or explaining, the representative actively engages the customer.

OVERCOMING THE MOST DREADED OBJECTIONS

There are some objections in particular that cause you to cringe or stutter or get ready for a fight. They challenge the very core of your business and what you do. They may sound something like this:

"Why should I buy from you? Your prices are too high."

"I'm happy with our current supplier. I see no reason to switch."

What to do? Don't dread them; be ready for them. In these special cases, the objection is so clear and straightforward that there's simply no need to clarify. Go right to acknowledging the objection, then prove or redirect as appropriate.

For example, when a customer throws this at you: "Why should I buy from you? Your prices are too high," you can respond with one of these:

"I understand your concern about the cost. Although our prices may be higher than some other suppliers, our quality and durability are superior to all others on the market."

"I understand your concern about price. Other customers expressed this concern at first, though they found that they get far more for their money because of our product's quality, durability, and value."

If a customer blocks you with this: "I'm happy with our current supplier. I see no reason to switch," you can respond with one of these:

"I appreciate your relationship with your current supplier. I would like to learn more about what you like about your supplier and what you want from this type of product."

"I recognize that you're happy with your current supplier. What you might not realize is that our products offer a wide range of enhancements that are not available elsewhere. Would you like to hear more about that?"

Experiment with MAGIC

Pair off with a colleague. Have one of you be the salesperson and the other, a customer. Acting out a sales scenario, practice incorporating The 33 Points. Reverse roles so that both of you get a feel for the two sides of the interaction. Practice all three sales scenarios: incoming calls, outgoing calls, and face-to-face meetings.

Next, score how well you did. Note where you did well and those areas that may benefit from additional practice. The more you use the principles in practice scenarios, the more natural they'll become once you're out there with customers and prospects.

A **MAGIC** Moment

One of our associates was surprised by a salesperson's listening skills and ability to find just the right bouquet for our associate's mother. Here's her story.

"Last Mother's Day, I opted to send my mother flowers for the occasion. I spent way too much time reviewing the flower catalogue and searching for the perfect bouquet that fit both my budget and my mother's tastes.

"When I finally called to place the order, the salesperson informed me that they were sold out of the pink tulip basket I had carefully selected. Discouraged, I went to another flower company and found a similar tulip arrangement. I was disheartened to hear that this bouquet was sold out too.

"But the salesperson's response surprised me: 'I am so sorry we are sold out. Was this for Mother's Day? I would love to help you find something else that would work.'

"And then, instead of just offering me another bouquet, she asked some probing questions: 'Did you want a pink bouquet, or was it the tulips that were important in this bouquet? You had selected a basket; is that what your mother wanted, or would a vase work just as well? Do you know where she was going to put it?'

"I answered her questions, and she listened carefully to my responses. There was a short pause, and she said, 'I've found a bouquet that sounds perfect. It has the pink flowers you want, and the size and price are comparable to your original choice. The only difference is that this one is in a vase instead of a basket, and it sounds like that would work better for your mother's dining room table anyway. How does that sound?'

"It sounded perfect. Perfect, because she hadn't just thrown out another choice—she had asked me what was important to me and listened to my responses to find a product that met my needs. She saved me time and energy, and helped me make a choice I felt great about."

FOLLOWING UP

Follow-up is a critical component of the sales process. It shows the customer that you care and that you value the relationship—that "out of sight, out of mind" is not your way of interacting. Little things can determine who gets the sale. A simple gesture—a handwritten thank-you note or an article of interest—shows a customer that you care.

Practice The Five MAGIC Steps and watch how your sales relationships transform. You'll win sales in the short term and build a foundation for long-term revenue and customer loyalty.

MAGIC **Maxims**

- MAGIC works to counter the negative associations people have with the idea of "sales" by placing the emphasis on building relationships and trust.

- To improve your sales results, focus on the customer's needs and goals— not just on your own goal of making a sale.

- To overcome objections, first clarify, then acknowledge, prove, or redirect.

chapter TWENTY-ONE

MAGIC in Collections
and Default Negotiations

When people think of collections, they tend to think of the classic "big club" approach: "Pay now, or else I'm going to bring out the big club and turn off your electricity, confiscate the item in question, or take away the family dog." Companies that use this threatening, competitive approach may achieve some short-term results, but at a significant long-term cost. In fact, this approach can cost them the relationship with that customer (and potential relationships with that customer's friends, coworkers, and neighbors). Simply put, this is the tragic approach.

This chapter is about a cooperative approach to collections and default negotiations, one that enables customers to leave with a positive feeling about the company. This approach builds trust, strengthens relationships, and yields win-win results.

THE TRAGIC APPROACH—COMPETITIVE

First, let's examine the "traditional" approach to collections and default negotiations in more detail. The standard approach has generally taken a confrontational or competitive tone: "You owe us three months' back mortgage payments. Pay within a week, or we foreclose."

The variations may differ somewhat, but the structure, tone, and message are generally consistent. They are very much in your face, in effect a sort of brinkmanship that threatens dire consequences if the other party doesn't act—and fast. Few people outside the realm of Al Capone feel comfortable with this approach.

This "our money or your kneecaps" strategy doesn't work, for a host of reasons. For one thing, it certainly doesn't make the other party want to have further contact with you.

On top of that, this competitive approach incorporates several other blunders:

- You're focusing on the person, not the issue: "*You'd* better pay . . ."

- You're focusing on your needs exclusively and not considering the other's as well: "We need that money."

- You're demanding rather than understanding. Who among us responds better to the former rather than the latter?

A **Tragic** Moment

A facilitator asked her class to share some of the competitive statements they've heard (or used) in negotiations of mortgage payments. Here is what the group came up with:

"I'm not your friend. If you want a friend, buy a dog."

"If you're not out of the house by Thursday, I'll be there on Friday with the sheriff!"

"You've been delinquent eight of the last ten months. Why should this time be any different?"

"You know you owe the money. Pay now or pay later."

"Do you like living outside?"

The whole class started laughing about these abrupt and somewhat absurd statements. This exercise broke the ice and got everyone thinking about the impact of their negotiation strategy. But it is no laughing matter that some people still use tragic phrases like these with their customers.

THE MAGIC APPROACH—COOPERATIVE

By contrast, a cooperative approach to these understandably awkward situations emphasizes a focus on mutual satisfaction with any outcome. Rather than one side's "winning" or "scoring points" at the other's expense, there's a focus on win-win solutions—on both parties coming away from the conversation with a sense that something beneficial to both has been accomplished.

In contrast to the competitive approach, a cooperative strategy emphasizes

- The issue, not the person involved

- Information concerning the context and content of the situation—the what and why that contribute to the issue that needs to be addressed

- Testing understanding rather than demanding

What stands out is that the cooperative approach achieves a real balance between maintaining the relationship with the customer and accomplishing the task at hand—collecting the amount due.

Be Prepared to Negotiate

MAGIC is about finding solutions—not establishing a winner and a loser. Along those lines, it's important to prepare to negotiate to arrive at a settlement that's appropriate for all parties involved.

The first thing to do is plan for the call. Have all the information you need readily available. Particularly important is any history or background with this customer. Think about how you wish to approach the conversation and set your objectives for the call.

Now you're ready for the most critical step of all: establishing the *bargaining arena*. Here's how you do it. First, identify what's known as your *most favored position*—the best possible outcome for you. This may be payment in full or a good share of what's owed. At the same time, you should earmark a settlement that for you is the minimum amount acceptable, also known as your *limit*. From there, think about those same two parameters for the person with whom you're dealing—what might be his range of acceptable amounts.

The bargaining arena is the common area where your two positions intersect and, therefore, offer the potential for a suitable solution. Note that a number of factors may come into play, such as the amount owed and the time frame in which it can be paid. But it's this shared dollar range that contains the best opportunity for a win-win outcome.

As you consider your position as well as the other person's potential response, put things into perspective. For instance, if a customer has had an excellent credit record for many years and has only encountered financial difficulties of late, then this information should affect your bargaining arena. So when talking with a customer, ask what has contributed to the issue at hand. It may be something such as a job loss, divorce, or serious illness—something that's beyond the person's control. That, too, can influence the bargaining arena and your negotiation methods.

Set the Tone Up Front

Just as with incoming calls, the greeting sets the tone of every outgoing collections call. Are you sending a "sledgehammer" signal or a professional relationship message?

Let's explore a few examples of tragic greetings. Do any sound familiar?

"Mr. Holtz, this is Abercrombie Company. I'm calling to let you know your bill is past due and to find out when you're going to pay."

"Ms. Johnson, Jeff from Pick Axe Collections. You haven't paid your bill in more than three months. What's going on?"

"Mr. Walton, you owe $1,260. You need to pay it now."

It's easy to see why these opening greetings start the call on a dubious track. They're unpleasant, abrupt, even a bit threatening. It's not hard to imagine why someone would react in a defensive manner (or even hang up!).

Contrast those with the following greetings:

"Mr. Mathews, this is Diane from Jones Mortgage. I am calling about your account that's now two months overdue. We value your solid credit record with us and would like to help you bring your account back into good standing."

"Good morning, Ms. Dubrowski. This is Jason Fenton from ABC Financial. I am calling regarding your February and March payments, which are past due. I want to help you get your account current."

"Good afternoon, Mr. Steiner. This is Marty Shea from Loan Corporation. We appreciate your business over the last ten years. I see that your account is thirty-six days past due. I'm calling to help you bring your account current."

These greetings are not merely positive in tone. They also place a clear emphasis on specific information—how much and how long the account is past due and how you can help. Energy isn't directed at finger pointing or blame, but rather on working toward a solution.

The customer is more likely to speak with you and work with you when you send a professional message from the very start.

Experiment with MAGIC

To help shift from the competitive to the cooperative approach, you can start by focusing on the words you use.

First, take a moment to list all the tragic phrases you have heard (or, dare we say, you have used) in collection calls. Here are some examples:

"You have to."

"Or else."

"You better . . ."

"This is your problem."

Put them all down and take a good look at them. Then make a commitment to stop using them and to use MAGIC phrases instead.

Next, your task is to write down as many cooperative phrases as you can that would be appropriate for collection calls. Here are a few to get you started:

"The best way I can help you . . ."

"May I suggest . . ."

"Let's review the options."

"I'd like to help."

See how many more you can come up with. Take a good look at that list and make a commitment to use these phrases even when the customer gets tense, resistant, or confrontational. These phrases will help you lead the call to an agreement, calmly and professionally. You might even post these phrases by your monitor so that they're handy when you need them.

NEGOTIATION TECHNIQUES

Whether you know it or not, we all negotiate all the time. No matter if it's deciding what to have for dinner or getting the kids to bed at a reasonable hour, we're all constantly involved in the give-and-take of negotiation.

Listen for Win-Win Solutions

Negotiation should be considered a positive means of structuring the communication process with an objective of a constructive outcome—for everyone involved, not just one person or party. You need to have not only goals in mind but also certain techniques at the ready—foremost of which is listening actively for opportunities to establish a win-win solution.

It's important to get the whole story so that you understand the real source of the issue. Not all customers want the same thing or are in the same boat. So ask questions and listen for the catchpoint. Doing so may not only enable you to identify the true focus of the issue but also give you a hint at a possible solution. For instance: if a customer has owed a certain amount of money for a long time, you may discover that he just obtained a new job after being out of work for a long period. Now you can work together on a payment plan.

Another element of active listening is paraphrasing, which helps you understand what the other person has said and, at the same time, lets her know that you understand. Paraphrasing is not blind parroting; it's an affirmation of understanding that can move the discussion toward resolution.

The following are some examples:

"So, you think a payment plan would work because . . ."

"As I understand it, your payment was delayed because . . ."

"So your new job will allow you to make greater payments instead of just interest charges?"

Empathize

Likewise, it's important to express empathy whenever appropriate. After all, many of these situations are difficult and charged with emotion. And you don't want to alienate a customer just because he's going through a tough time.

Often, people who owe money feel very much alone—as if they're twisting in the wind with no one there to offer them a hand. One way to address this anxiety is to let them know that you recognize this fact. For example:

"I understand that this is a difficult time for you. I'd like to work with you to develop a payment plan."

"I'm sure this has been tough on you. I'd like to help. Let's work on this together."

Letting the other person know that you care and are willing to work with them builds trust. And people tend to work with those they trust, not with those who treat them as criminals.

Present Benefits

Many people think that you need to threaten or hang dire consequences over the other person's head to succeed at negotiation. Not true! These methods may not work at all. Even if they do lead to an agreement, it is short term at best and leaves the person with a "bad feeling" about you and your organization.

So how do you influence the other party to see your perspective and accept your offer? It's all about benefits—or, put another way, it's about letting her see what's in it for her. Once she understands how your offer will benefit her, she is far more likely to shift her thinking and move your way.

What kinds of benefits can you share? Here are just a few:

- Avoidance of credit problems and their aftereffects
- Savings (for example, lower interest costs or lower payments)
- Continuation or extension of service
- Convenience

Here's what a benefit statement might sound like:

"Mr. Hanks, if you pay down your bill as discussed, you'll save $900 in interest charges."

"If you pay $120 this month, Mr. Eldorado, your service will continue uninterrupted."

The idea is to establish a reason why the other party should say yes to your offer. In the end, you'll have a solution that both parties feel positive about.

Let the Customer Make the First Move

One of the most effective ways to move toward resolution is to let the customer make the first offer. You already know your own comfort level; it's imperative that you know his as well. So solicit his position. For instance:

"I see that you owe $3,463.27. What amount can you send today?"

"I see that you have not paid our bill for forty-five days. What can you do to keep your account in good standing?"

In this manner, you get a sense of where the customer is and how far he may be willing to move from his initial position. At that point, you are in control and can take the lead.

This is far more effective than when you make the first move, which can put you behind the eight ball, as you'll see here:

You: I see that you owe $3,463.27. Can you pay $2,500 today?

Customer: Oh no, I can't do that. I told you, I'm out of work!

You: Well, can you pay $2,000?

Customer: No—I don't think I can pay that much. I'm in a real bind.

You: Ah . . . OK . . . How about . . .

So be sure to let the customer make the first offer, and you'll have a better chance of getting more money sooner.

Handle Objections and Excuses

MAGIC doesn't mean letting a customer who's behind on her bills get away with anything. Far from it—yet it does mean being ready to handle any objection or excuse that a caller may express. Resist the temptation to argue or rationalize your position. Instead, start with agreement and empathy, then move on to suggest appropriate solutions. For example:

"I understand your concern about your statement, and I'm here to help."

"I realize that you've had some challenges lately, and I'd like to help ensure that your credit remains strong."

"I understand that this is a difficult time for you right now. Other customers in similar situations have found that making a payment now will help their credit standing in the long run."

When customers throw excuses at you, don't let the conversation end just yet. Ask questions so that you can move to the next step. For example:

If the Customer Says . . .	You Can Respond Like This:
"I promise to pay."	Get a specific date that the payment will be made.
"My income is slow right now."	Ask when he expects his income to improve.
"That person is not available."	Ask when she'll be available for a callback.

A **MAGIC** Moment

A facilitator shared this story about an influential participant in one of his classes:

"I was teaching a MAGIC Approach to Collections program to an experienced group from an automotive company.

"I was surprised to hear them talk about the number of customers that defaulted on their lease or finance payments. Seven out of the group of eight joked about the number of these 'deadbeats' they were dealing with. These seven were young bucks who felt that the only way they could collect the company's money was by playing the tough guy and threatening the deadbeats. There was a fair amount of resistance to the cooperative approach to collections, which involved developing relationships versus burning them.

"For the first half of day one of the class, the eighth participant sat quietly, watching the interaction. He had twenty years of experience in the business and was letting people air their views. (Kind of like the experienced cowboy watching a fight, chewing on his toothpick.)

"Once he understood the cooperative principles and could see the resistance I was meeting, he spoke his piece: 'This man knows what he is talking about, and it is worth each of you taking note. The style of collecting he is teaching us is exactly what I use, and the reason for my success. Try it out, and you'll see.'

"His annual collections were more than twice any other collector's. The others had assumed his success was because he was a tough guy. He set them straight when he declared, 'It is all in the approach. Build the relationship, and the money will follow.'"

PUTTING IT ALL TOGETHER

Now that we've covered the principles of cooperative collections and specific techniques to achieve win-win solutions, it's time to put them all together. There are five steps and 33 Points of MAGIC collections and default negotiations, as shown in Exhibit 21.1. Remember that every outbound call can affect the impression you make and, ultimately, your bottom line.

Exhibit 21.1: The 33 Points of MAGIC Collections and Default Negotiations

Make a Connection: Create a Professional Impression

1. Greeting: Offer welcoming words.
2. Greeting: Maintain an upbeat tone.
3. Greeting: Use an unhurried pace.
4. Use the customer's name as soon as you hear it.
5. Present the purpose of the call.
6. Highlight the customer's account history.
7. Tell the customer you will help.
8. Ask permission to gain more information.

Exhibit 21.1: The 33 Points of MAGIC Collections and Default Negotiations

Act Professionally: Express Courtesy and Confidence

9. Be courteous: Use "please" and "thank you."

10. Show a sincere, helpful attitude through tone.

11. Build trust by remaining calm.

12. Express appropriate empathy through words.

13. Express appropriate empathy through tone.

Get to the Heart of the Matter: Listen and Ask Questions

14. Ask questions to find the catchpoint(s) and the reason for default.

15. Repeat numbers and clarify spelling.

16. Avoid tragic phrases and jargon.

17. Use "I," not "we," when appropriate.

18. Cooperate, don't compete.

19. Listen and rephrase effectively.

Interpret and Clarify: Highlight What You Will Do

20. Give security using MAGIC phrases; demonstrate understanding.

21. Be knowledgeable and accurate; establish the bargaining arena.

22. Keep the call to an appropriate length; be specific.

23. Be proactive: Set a deadline; offer a solution.

24. Speak clearly with proper volume and pace.

25. Respond to objections.

26. Summarize the next step(s).

Close with Agreement: End on a Professional Note

27. Get agreement on the next step(s).

28. Use the customer's name.

29. End with a MAGIC phrase.

30. Close with a sincere tone.

31. Let the customer hang up first.

32. Did you lead the call professionally?

33. Are you closer to a settlement?

MAGIC **Maxims**

- Avoid the "traditional" method of confrontation or competition when involved in collections or default negotiations; it's notoriously ineffective for the long term.

- Use a cooperative approach—show that you wish to work with the customer rather than against him.

- Express empathy when appropriate and focus on the issue at hand, not the person involved.

- Ask questions and listen to details so that you can offer appropriate suggestions to achieve win-win solutions.

PART SIX

MAGIC
in Real Life

Personal Stories
and Lessons for Life

I t has probably occurred to you that the principles in this book can
apply to everyday situations as well—whether you're at the dry
cleaner, your son's school, the grocery store, or your neighbor's house.
Indeed they can. And when you bring MAGIC to every interaction,
you will be amazed at the results.

Here are some real-life stories from people who have used our approach in their
personal lives. Many have had their lives improved, if not downright transformed,
by the connection they experienced.

GOING THE EXTRA MILE

The Memory Maker

I was getting ready to go home when I noticed a couple peeking into
the sales area. I asked if I could help, and the lady snapped "No!" I
could tell that something was wrong. I said, "My name is Connie, and
I am a manager here. You seem upset; are you sure I can't help you
with something?" At this point the woman burst into tears and started
yelling about a picture. I escorted her to a nearby couch and asked her
to sit down and explain.

She and her husband were owners and guests in our resort. In tears
she explained that she and her husband had had their picture taken in

our complimentary photo area. They were told by member services that they would get an 8"×10" photo, and they only got a 5"×7". Now this may seem quite unimportant, but to this guest it was major.

I took their 5"×7" photo and walked over to the member services desk. The agent explained that their printer no longer made 8"×10" photos. They had changed the printer the day before, but the sign by the photo area still stated 8"×10". There were no other photo printers available.

Due to the level of dissatisfaction of the guest, I asked the concierge to do an errand for me. I gave him $10 and asked him to go to a local drug store where I knew there was a photo enlargement machine. I asked him to make me an 8"×10" of the 5"×7" photo, put it in a frame, and deliver it to the guest room with some chocolates.

I then went back to the couple and explained what was happening and that they would have their 8"×10" photo within the hour. They left to go back to their room, thanking me for all I had done.

As I walked away, the gentleman came back up and tapped me on the shoulder. He thanked me again and said, "I just have to apologize for my wife and explain. We are from Louisiana. We just lost everything in Hurricane Katrina. Our home and every one of our photos was destroyed. Today is our forty-fourth wedding anniversary, and this was to be our first photo together. I can imagine this seems very insignificant to you, but this photo meant everything to my wife. Thank you. We will always remember this trip and this photo." As I walked away, I got tears in my eyes and realized we truly are "Memory Makers."

Do the Right Thing

Doing things right and doing the right thing. . . . I struggled a lot to figure out the difference between these two phrases the very first time that one of my supervisors mentioned this to me. . . .

Earlier this year, one of our members called Community Health Group to speak to one of our representatives. After two rings, one of our very committed and passionate employees answered the phone. On the other side of the phone was "Janet," a desperate single woman with very limited financial resources. Janet called to request services for her teenage son, a lonely, suicidal teenager who suffered from severe depression. "Eddie" had no insurance coverage. Now if you have ever been in the position of having to tell a needy person that their health plan does not cover what they need, you know how difficult this call can be. Yet the job of our employees is to do things right.

And that is exactly what George Scolari, a behavioral health services supervisor who has been with us for five years, did. He informed the member that these services weren't covered because her son was not a covered member under CHG. Now, ordinarily for any other health plan employee, the call ends there. But not for George. For George, that is the beginning. Why? Because George doesn't just do things right—he does the right thing. He knew that simply telling Janet that we couldn't cover services for a nonmember wasn't enough. He knew that members ordinarily know that seeking coverage for someone who is not covered by the health plan is bound to get a No answer. What this told George is that this mother must have been desperate to have even placed this call—desperate to find an answer.

So George went to work, used his resources and influence to help this member out. Within two hours Eddie was in an anger management course at a cost of $15. What George did for this member was to give her noncovered son access to health care, in a culturally sensitive manner and at a cost that she could afford. Would she have been able to do this on her own? Perhaps. But it may have taken days to figure out the system, and that may have been too late to benefit her suicidal son.

The story doesn't end there. That same evening, Janet made a call to George to let him know that Eddie had just come home from the anger management class and that he couldn't stop talking about the experience and how it had changed his life. This class gave a very angry young man and his mother hope. Hope that with the right treatment he could change his life.

Now, we are a health plan, and we are in the business of selling insurance coverage, not hope. However, hope is one of those gifts that our employees give our members simply by knowing that what they do on a daily basis affects the community we serve. And that is precisely what has made us unique and successful for the past twenty years—twenty years of employees like George Scolari who know that serving our community takes more than doing things right. It also means that we need to do the right thing not only for our members but for our community. I knew that George had done the right thing for Janet when I had the opportunity to listen to her voicemail message to George. Listening to her was like listening to someone who had received a few moments of relief from pain that she had been enduring for years. Is there anything "more right" than throwing out a life preserver to a grieving person and bringing her back to shore?

THE LEGACY OF MAGIC

The Great Customer Service Game

When my children were young, we would play the "Great Customer Service" game. Here is how it worked. After we finished shopping at the mall, we would spend our ride home talking about the great service we got at each place we went into. At times they wanted to talk about the bad service, and I would remind them that this was the Great Customer Service game, not the Bad Customer Service game.

What was interesting is that they could pick up on the littlest things. One day we were at a watch store trying to get new batteries in a number of wristwatches. The store didn't normally do this for customers. This particular evening, the salesperson said that it was slow and that in between customers she would replace them for us. When we returned about an hour later, they were all done. I paid her for the batteries and then I proceeded to give her a tip, which she refused. She said, "I am glad to help people, and if more of them were nice and understanding like you were to me, I would do things like this more often."

When we got in the car, the boys expressed their amazement that she didn't take the money. They also noticed that when we first went into the store, the salesperson had a mad look on her face, and when we left the store with the watches, she was smiling.

Because of this game, our sons pick up on great customer service all the time. Once when Sean was about eleven years old, he said that I better give the waitress a big tip because she gave me great customer service. I missed something and asked what she had done to get a big tip. He told me that she had filled up my iced tea glass without my even asking. Well, I hadn't even noticed this, and it sparked another opportunity to discuss great customer service—service that often goes unnoticed and unappreciated. I made a point of saying thank you when she returned to our table, and I gladly gave her a big tip.

A Long-Awaited Reconciliation

For a good part of my early adult years, I consciously chose not to vote as a sort of rebellion against what I saw as the pathetic state of the U.S. political body. Many political discussions have transpired over the last thirteen years with my father, and much disagreement was openly displayed by both of us, much more frequent than I care to admit. I had always assumed Dad was a staunch Republican, and Dad had assumed I was an avid Democrat.

It was after a training session I ran in 2005 that I realized that my relationship with my own father, whom I loved deeply, was threaded with implied disrespect whenever the subject of politics arose. So I decided to use the skills I had learned with dear old Dad.

The results were utterly amazing! My mom witnessed the entire encounter and—I think—was dumbfounded when Dad and I admitted that we are both registered as Independents and always have been. He shared the reasons he votes as he does, how he feels about the state of the world, and why he feels that way. I heard and understood him and then he listened rationally to my reasons for voting as I do, and how I feel about the world and why. I have a newfound respect for my father, and I believe he does for me as well. I now look forward to political discussions, and plan to use my MAGIC skills to keep us fully engaged.

Double the MAGIC

On any given morning, my three-year-old twins are taken from their restful beds and strapped into their car seats for the short drive to my mother's house to spend the day while I work. This morning was no different. Normally, because they are sleepy, I carry them into the house, one at a time. This morning, however, I had a few other things to carry in at Mom's, so I began a dialogue with the twins to warm them up to the idea of walking in rather than being carried.

Race piped up and said, "OK, Mommy, we will walk in." Looking in my rearview mirror, I said, "Why, thank you, Race!" With a smile on his face and a gleam in his eye, my freckle-faced three-year-old exclaimed, "My pleasure!" Oh, the joy of MAGIC! Maybe MAGIC should stand for Make A Great Impression on your Children!

The Value of Listening, Not Lecturing

One afternoon, when our daughter was a sophomore in high school, I picked her up after field hockey practice. She was in tears and looked downtrodden. I asked her what the matter was.

She was totally bummed because they had chosen captains for the team and she had not been picked. Even though she had four more years of experience than anyone else on the team, they chose someone who was a rookie, but more popular with her teammates. It just didn't seem fair.

My first thought was to say, "Get a life! You can still give your best to the team and make a huge contribution." Instead, I listened to what she was saying and responded with this: "Wow, I can totally relate. My junior year in college, I was one of the best soccer players on the team, and I was not chosen for captain either. Instead, they chose a senior who was a good baseball player, but not very good at soccer, but a really funny guy. It stunk."

And then I did the hardest thing. I shut up. I let us sit in silence as we drove home. After about two minutes (which seemed like an hour), she said, "You know, it may not be that bad . . . I mean, I can still make a difference on the team, and we can still have a great season."

Wow, did I learn a lesson. Instead of chiding her, I communicated to her that I understood what she was going through and how she was feeling. She felt listened to and valued, so it freed her up to think about the situation in a way that was constructive. I was grateful for sharing that special but difficult moment with her!

THE MAGIC CONNECTION

What You Do unto Others . . .

I tell people that I get great service most places I do business. It is because I look at each person as my customer even when I am the customer.

Businesses know me by name, they will call me if there is a problem, and on occasion they will waive a late fee or give me a sweater cleaned for free. I believe this occurs because of the relationship I have built with them.

What was really cool is that about six months ago our eldest son, Colby, was home from college and went to rent some videos. When he got home he said, "Mom, I love the relationships you have established in town. When I went into Video Exchange, the owner asked me how school was going. I was so surprised that he knew who I was and that I was away at school. We chatted for a while, he made some recommendations, and told me to say hello to you. It was pretty cool being recognized and getting such personalized service."

What touched me is that my son got exceptional service because of the connection I had made. Boy, someone treating my son with such care; I will always continue to do business there.

Toll Talk

I was in Denver one day and went through three tollbooths on my way to the hotel.

Tollbooth 1: On my first trip, I approached the tollbooth with the efficiency of a track runner handing off a baton in a relay race. My arm was stretched out the window ready to hand off the dollar bill, and I was expecting in the same motion to receive forty cents change and a receipt.

Not at this tollbooth. The first thing I noticed was a white nameplate that had the name "Martha" and an American flag embroidered in red and blue. I noticed there were even white stars on the flag.

I looked up at a sweet, grandmotherly woman as she said, "Good evening, sir. Would you like a receipt today?" Her voice was as welcoming as if I were at the front door of her home.

Without responding, I looked down at the nameplate again for a few seconds. Then she asked, "Would you like some fries with that burger?"

I smiled. "Not today, thanks. But I will take that receipt."

"All right then. You have a good night."

It was 9:30 at night, and I thought about how many people she must see in a day and wondered if she was that friendly with everyone. She was exceptional.

Tollbooth 2: I slowed down for this one. There was another nameplate. This one was stained light brown, and "Mark" was engraved in the wood.

Mark said, "Good evening. Would you like a receipt tonight?"

"Yes, please," I replied.

"Are you coming from the airport?"

"Yes, I am."

"Must be a late night for you."

"Yup."

"Well then, drive safely; good night."

"Thanks, goodnight."

Tollbooth 3: Now I was really curious. This time the nameplate was white cardboard, and the name "Robert" was written in brown marker.

Robert said, "Good evening. Would you like a receipt?"

I replied, "Sure, but can I ask you a question? I've been to three tollbooths tonight, and each person was so friendly. I'm not used to this; most people I see in tollbooths are grumpy."

He responded, "If anyone here was a grump, he wouldn't be here for very long."

"Really? Does that mean that you are evaluated?"

"Well, it's expected that we be friendly, but how could you possibly keep doing this if it made you feel grumpy?"

On subsequent trips, I went on E-470 during rush hour in the mornings and afternoons. Surely I expected to meet some grumps during these busy hours.

There were a few people who didn't smile much, but they didn't seem grumpy. They each had handmade nameplates at their booths, and each person looked me in the eyes and asked if I'd like a receipt. Each one said, "Have a good day" as I was leaving.

Hmmm. It made me want to talk to the "tollbooth manager." And I can only imagine how he might greet me at his office door: "Good afternoon. Would you like a cup of coffee?"

PUT ON A HAPPY FACE

MAGIC Goes to the Dogs

When I was holding a MAGIC class last year, one of the participants showed up on the second day of class with a story about how she had used her training.

Adrienne was having difficulty with a neighbor and the neighbor's dog. The dog barked a great deal, so she and the neighbor were not on the best of terms.

When she got home after the first day of the training, she decided to call her neighbor to see if they could talk and work out the situation. She invited her neighbor (and her dog) over for a glass of wine. (No wine for the dog.)

She listened and used empathy with the situation. The neighbor explained that the dog was alone through the day a lot, and the neighbor felt this was a problem. Because Adrienne was semiretired, she and her neighbor decided that when Adrienne was home, she would talk to the dog and let it come over and play with her own dog.

Adrienne was relieved and happy that she had applied her newly learned skills with a positive result. Weeks later, Adrienne told me that she, her neighbor, and their dogs had become great friends and that they walked their dogs together in the evenings.

The "Sticker People"

My husband and I take cute stickers when we go out to eat. We ask the waiters their name and how they are doing that day. If we receive service with a smile and courtesy, we give the waiter a smile sticker and words of praise! The smiles, looks of surprise, and happy responses are heart warming.

We often forget that waiters and waitresses have difficult face-to-face interactions and don't expect customers to care about their day. We are well known at our favorite restaurant and hear "Here come the sticker people!" when we walk in! This has allowed us to make warm friendships and receive great service every time!

A RANDOM ACT OF MAGIC

A Good Deed

I was crossing the street one day when I found a large black binder in the middle of the road. I asked my associate, Lilli, to see if we had any visitors to our office that morning. She said no, but offered to try to find out who the binder belonged to.

When I opened it up, I realized it was someone's appointment book, and I knew that it was important. Much to my surprise, we were able to track down the owner of the binder, who was thrilled that someone had found it. We learned that the appointment book had been stolen out of his car and evidently discarded on the road right in front of our office.

He offered to pay to have it shipped back, but once I learned that he lived in Fairfield (as do I), I offered to return the book to him that evening. He said he would be out that night and suggested it would be too much trouble for me to return the book the next morning. I assured him that it would be my pleasure, and we arranged a time for me to deliver the book to him.

He was totally overwhelmed with the effort that had been made for a total stranger. I was happy to see the look of relief on his face and to know that I helped someone in need.

A MAGIC TRANSFORMATION

A Profound Change

I work at a resort in the Walt Disney World area. When we first began the MAGIC training, the general manager invited all of the department managers to participate. I don't think he understood the profound impact that simple decision was going to have.

Soon after the MAGIC classes, we began MAGIC Moments, a fifteen-minute MAGIC session every day. The hourly staff for operations, housekeeping, and security all participated.

One particular housekeeper named Maria was an excellent worker. Everything was always spotless, she always had a smile on her face, and she did her job with pride. She was also very quiet, and seemed a little distant.

Eventually, after attending MAGIC Moment sessions, she began to open up, with a simple "Good morning," every morning. Soon, we would hear "May I help you with anything else?"

Then the really amazing happened.

She stopped me, the facilitator on the property, and said, "I would like to thank you."

"What for?" I asked.

"Thank you for bringing MAGIC to me. I have noticed such a change in everyone at this property. Everyone says hello and good morning, and I love it. I have so much fun in the class, and I even use it on my husband and son. Before, I was invisible to everyone, and now, I feel I am a part of everyone."

Then she hugged me and again told me how much she loved it, and how much it made her love her job.

Maria is now a part of the operations team and recently was awarded the Employee of the Month, an award that was truly earned. She continually demonstrates MAGIC qualities in everything she does, in her job and in her life.

Some Final Thoughts

People can't read each other's minds. Nor can any person ever know exactly how another is feeling. Nonetheless, we hope that by this point in the book you have become convinced that every communication, no matter how small or seemingly insignificant, has the potential to make a world of difference.

Of course, the type of impact your interactions have on people depends on your mind-set. In just one short moment, you have the ability to make a MAGIC connection with someone, just as you have the ability to make a tragic one.

In the end, how you live in your world has to do with your choice as a professional—and as a person—to make a connection with others.

Once you make the choice to build and strengthen your relationships, it only gets easier from there. With The Five MAGIC Steps, you can ensure that every communication has a positive impact. Let's review them one more time:

M   Make a Connection: Build the Relationship

A   Act Professionally: Express Confidence

G   Get to the Heart of the Matter: Listen and Ask Questions

I   Inform and Clarify What You Will Do

C   Close with the Relationship in Mind

Throughout the book, we have given you versions of these steps for a wide range of situations, such as incoming and outgoing calls, face-to-face contacts, sales, and collections. Using these steps as your compass, you can't help but improve your customer's experience. However, if you go a little further and adopt MAGIC as a mind-set, you will accomplish something far greater. With more effective communication skills, stronger relationships, and a true concern for other individuals, you will contribute to the improvement of our society as a whole—something that, believe it or not, you have the tools to achieve.

Because whose responsibility is it really to make this world a place in which we all like to live? It's yours. It's ours. It's everyone's. And now that you have the skills and knowledge, there's no better time to improve the norm.

To leave you thinking about the choices you make, we'd like to share just one more inspirational story:

A Gift from a Stranger

A colleague was driving home from work one evening when he noticed a crew of laborers building a stone wall. It was summer, and at about 6 PM it was just cooling off from what some might call a scorcher of a day. He had noticed the men there ten hours earlier, and here they still were, building that wall.

The next morning, our colleague decided to do the unexpected. As he neared the wall the next morning, he slowed down and pulled over to the side of the road. Bearing a twelve-pack of ice-cold spring water, he approached one of the men. He then smiled and handed the man the water, saying, "These are for you and your friends."

The man at first looked a bit startled. Then, realizing that this was a gift from a stranger, he returned the smile and simply said, "Gracias!" He then began handing out the water bottles to his fellow workers, as our colleague went on with his day.

So there you have it. Five simple steps, one gold standard. So many unforgettable moments. We hope we have given you something to think about. And, the next time you interact with someone, you may just choose to make it MAGIC.

ACKNOWLEDGMENTS

A book like this comes from the heart—we love what we do. We truly believe in MAGIC, and love sharing it with others and seeing the difference it makes. This book also comes from thousands of conversations, relationships, and experiences we've had in the twenty-plus years we have worked together. There are so many people who have inspired us, taught us, and collaborated with us along the way. They are really the ones responsible for this book. So, to be true to MAGIC principles, we want to acknowledge and thank them, for we could not have written this book without them.

We'd first like to acknowledge our associates at Communico; they are a special group of people. They have a passion to serve and a commitment to make the world a better place. They don't just "do" MAGIC, they *are* MAGIC. Very special thanks go to Jean Marie Johnson. She worked tirelessly along with us to ensure that the words in the book really captured the essence of MAGIC. She spent countless hours pouring over the manuscript with us; she was always there for us whenever we needed a boost. We can't thank her enough for her feedback, suggestions, and dedication to the project.

We'd also like to thank Anne Koproski, who managed the whole process so that we stayed on track; Steve Lamm and Jerry Walsh, our lead MAGIC consultants who shared their vast experience and their stories with us; and Kathy Andersen, Evelyn Jones, Steve Loso, and Bill Salvador for their patience with us in the process and for being there when we needed them. Last, our thanks go to Sandy Wilder, our partner and the leader of Communico. He helped create the vision for this book and cheered us on to make it a reality.

Our gratitude goes to our clients for choosing MAGIC and for supporting its concepts. With their help, MAGIC has made a measurable difference; they have embraced a service mind-set and stand out from the rest. Equally important are the certified MAGIC facilitators in those organizations. Their commitment and enthusiasm for MAGIC has helped spread a real spirit of exceptional service in their organizations.

There are also our independent contractors who are models of MAGIC as they travel around the globe. They are Joyce Bailey, Gregg Barratt, Robyn Batts, Liza Clouse, Grace Dennison, Mary Ann Dirickson, Max Gage, Wally Hauck, Connie Kelly, Rich Kuepper, Cheryl Kuhn, Patty Mathieu, Brian Cole Miller, Burke Miller, Paula Sherwin, and Shannon Swift.

The MAGIC and Tragic Moments are our favorite parts of the book. We hope you like them too. Many Communico associates and independent contractors contributed heartfelt stories to this book. Real-life stories were also submitted by the following colleagues and clients: Dotty Baker, Monica Bignelli, Nicole Bovey, Lisa Davis, Casey Estling, Stephen Fleck, Judith Hamer, Kathy Harvey, Susan Korthals, Darrell Maness, Gary McNulty, Andy Negrete, Sherry Payne, Carol Ragon, Meg Reilly, Laurisa Sampson, Ann Warren, and Jennifer Yelton.

John Doerr and Mike Schultz of the Wellesley Hills Group deserve special attention. They knew about our dream to write a book and helped us make it happen. They have been unfailingly supportive of our efforts. Their experience, counsel, and friendship have been invaluable. They also introduced us to Becca Gould, who provided the last bit of inspiration we needed to finish the book.

Thanks to Jeff Wuorio for educating us about the writing process and helping us put our thoughts on paper. We are also grateful for Neal Maillet, editor at Jossey-Bass, who believed in the concept when he first heard about it and helped others see its potential. Our thanks also go to Mary Garrett and Michele Jones for their watchful eyes throughout the editing process, and to everyone else at Jossey-Bass who helped shepherd this book from its early stages to its present form.

Finally, we are grateful to our families, who keep us humble and are a constant reminder of the MAGIC in this world.

Diane Berenbaum, a senior vice president and owner of Communico Ltd., has helped foster and build strong, long-lasting client relationships for the company.

Diane's work in the fields of marketing, communication, and customer service training and development spans more than twenty-five years. She continues to work with a large array of clients in a variety of industries. She has partnered with many leading companies, including Anthem BCBS, Convergys Corporation, K. Hovnanian Homes, Aon Corporation, Evenflo, Johns Hopkins HealthCare, Liberty Mutual, Fairfield Resorts, and ABN AMRO Bank (Switzerland).

Diane has authored and coauthored numerous articles and has delivered training and coaching services to both senior leadership teams and front-line associates.

Diane holds an M.B.A. from Northwestern's Kellogg School of Management and a B.S. in business administration from the University of North Carolina at Chapel Hill.

Tom Larkin, a senior vice president and owner of Communico Ltd., is an authority on customer service initiatives and customer relations training and development.

Tom's work in the training and education field spans more than twenty-two years. He continues to work with senior leadership teams in a variety of industries. Tom has been interviewed on both radio and television concerning communication skills and customer relations. He has personally worked with many leading service companies, including JPMorgan Chase, CitiMortgage, ING Financial, Anthem BCBS, Colgate-Palmolive, Pepsico, and the New York Stock Exchange.

Tom has worked with companies in Europe and has recently consulted with call centers in India to provide quality monitoring programs for one of the world's leading banks.

Tom has presented at several industry-leading conferences and symposiums, including the Gartner Summit, International Contact Center Management (ICCM), the Call Center Exchange, Call Center Network Group (CCNG), and others. He was also selected as a moderator for the White House Conference on Small Business for the state of Connecticut.

Tom holds a B.A. in communication arts with a minor in marketing from Arizona State and an M.A. in counseling psychology from Lewis and Clark. He is currently a faculty member with Fairfield University's Department of Communication.

ABOUT COMMUNICO LTD.

Communico Ltd. is a customer service training and consulting company that partners with organizations to help them build and sustain exceptional service cultures. We believe that *Making A Great Impression on the Customer (MAGIC®)* is one of the greatest leverage points organizations can use to increase revenue, reduce costs, and improve employee and customer satisfaction and retention.

Over the last twenty-eight years, we have worked with a wide range of companies, including Anthem BCBS, Bank of America, Citigroup, Colgate Palmolive, EMC Corporation, Georgia-Pacific, ING Financial, Johns Hopkins HealthCare, Pepsico, UnumProvident Companies, Wells Fargo, and Zale Corporation.

Please visit us at www.CommunicoLtd.com or call 1-800-777-8241.